Understanding
Learning
Styles

Making a Difference for Diverse Learners

Authors

Kelli Allen, Jeanna Scheve, and Vicki Nieter

Foreword by Gregory J. Kaiser

SHELL EDUCATION

Publishing Credits

Dona Herweck Rice, *Editor-in-Chief*; Lee Aucoin, *Creative Director*; Don Tran, *Print Production Manager;* Timothy J. Bradley, *Illustration Manager*; Lori Kamola, M.S. Ed., *Editorial Director*; Wendy Conklin, M.A., Hillary Wolfe, *Editors*; Lee Aucoin, *Cover Designer;* Robin Erickson, *Interior Layout Designer;* Corinne Burton, M.S. Ed., *Publisher*

Shell Education
5301 Oceanus Drive
Huntington Beach, CA 92649-1030
http://www.shelleducation.com
ISBN 978-1-4258-0046-8
© 2011 Shell Educational Publishing, Inc.
Reprinted 2012

Table of Contents

Classroom teachers desiring to maximize their students' learning will find *Understanding Learning Styles: Making a Difference for Diverse Learners* by Kelli Allen, Jeanna Scheve, and Vicki Nieter a very useful and practical guide to effectively differentiating their classroom instruction. Throughout my years of elementary school teaching, I always sensed that my students had unique characteristics as learners, but struggled to first accurately identify individual learner needs and then to find the know-how, time, and energy to plan and prepare lessons to meet those needs on a daily basis. *Understanding Learning Styles: Making a Difference for Diverse Learners*, as the title suggests, approaches differentiating instruction with a focus on the practical application of learning styles theory to classroom teaching. Had I read such a book when I was an elementary school teacher, meeting the instructional needs of all of my students would have been much easier.

The usefulness of this book for classroom teachers lies in the practical application of four well-respected learning style paradigms, including perhaps the most well-known learning styles theory of Multiple Intelligences developed by Howard Gardner. Each of the four models is concisely summarized, followed by a section titled "Application of this model for everyday classroom use and lesson planning." This section of each chapter provides the reader with categorical descriptions of student characteristics, preferred learning strategies and learning products, and a description of what students do best within each identified learning style. The practical classroom application comes from the authors' descriptions of the types of instructional focus proven to be effective for each learning style and a clear, concise description of each learner type, titled "Student profile." Each learning theory chapter concludes with a section called "Sample activities for each learning style" that models for the reader activities designed to match and enhance each learning style.

The four learning styles theories are further applied to the classroom in Chapter 5, "Assessing Learning Styles." Each of the theory's assessment instruments are described and applied to classroom learning. To fully understand each instrument's instructional application, teachers are encouraged to complete the assessment surveys. Information on how to secure access to these instruments is provided.

Perhaps the most useful and encouraging part of the book for classroom teachers seeking to apply learning style theory to their classroom instruction is found in Chapter 6, "The Yes I Can! Model of Organizing Teaching Within These Learning Styles." This chapter describes the development of Individualized Learning Plans that account for individual student learning style preferences, followed by procedures for implementing these plans, sample activities, and finally, assessment ideas. The book concludes with sample forms suggesting ways to successfully develop, implement, and assess these Individualized Learning Plans.

After reading this wonderfully practical book addressing the challenge of meeting the diverse learning needs of all students, I came away with an appreciation for its compassionate approach towards both teachers and students. The authors successfully met their book's dual objective of articulating the need to understand and apply learning style theory to classroom instruction as a vehicle for meeting the instructional needs of all students and the practical challenges teachers face when working to effectively differentiate their instruction.

Gregory J. Kaiser
Multiple Subject Credential Program Director
Department of Teacher Education
Azusa Pacific University

If you are reading this, you are most likely in the education field at some level, whether it be in teaching, mentoring, or administration. Try to remember when you were sitting where your students are now. Were there times that you felt anxious, ill-prepared, or confused by content that just didn't make sense to you? Maybe you went to another teacher or a peer who explained the content differently, drew a picture, or used props, and finally, you got it! It was probably not that you were incapable of grasping the content, but possibly that the approach used to provide the necessary information was ineffective. In this time of outcomes-based and high-stakes assessments, it is crucial that the most efficient approaches be used in every classroom and with every student. This book offers multiple ways you can rise to the challenge and enhance your classroom with innovative and research-based techniques that will appeal to each learner's strengths.

Every classroom consists of individuals with diverse strengths, backgrounds, and approaches to learning. Understanding and responding to each student's individual learning style can be challenging for teachers. This book will introduce various learning styles, the research behind each style, and how to use this information to engage students in learning activities that are best suited for them. We will discuss numerous types of learning styles and provide practical strategies that enhance learning according to each style.

Learning styles and today's student

What is meant by *learning styles*? A variety of different answers exists, but a formal response is that a learning style is a preferred way of thinking, processing, and understanding information. Each person prefers a pattern of thought and behavior that influences his or her learning process. In other words, we all learn in different ways. You might ask, "If that's *learning style*, then what is *teaching style*?" The *teaching style* is the way instructors teach. Most teachers are chronological, systematic presenters, but the majority of their students do not learn this way. Knowing this information, it is essential to alter teaching strategies to meet the needs of all students. In other words, if students cannot learn the way we teach them, then we must teach them the way they learn best.

Current educational reform involves changing the classroom from a teacher-centered to a student-centered environment. It is old-fashioned and archaic to see the teacher as the provider of all knowledge, with students simply learning the information in whichever way the teacher chooses to present it. For many years, educators have known that students learn by different means. But, we are finally beginning to change the way that we teach to encompass these different learning styles.

This generation of students has more resources available to them at their fingertips than any previous generation. As a society, we revel in the freedom of choice to have just about anything tailored to our exact needs and wants, from fast food restaurants to customized cell phone plans. To meet the demanding needs of today's extremely diverse learners, teachers need activities that utilize current technological applications and are tailored to each individual's personal learning styles.

Every child is born with the capability to learn. Yet children (and adults) generally have a preferred style in which they learn best. A student may learn through a combination of styles, but usually he or she favors one learning style over others.

For example:

- You may be able to spell by visualizing a word, but your students may not be able to memorize spelling words unless they write them down first.
- Your students may prefer making a model to demonstrate a concept rather than writing a description of the concept.

There is no right or wrong learning style. A teacher's primary learning style may be different from his or her student's learning style(s). For a teacher to work effectively with a student, the teacher needs to understand his or her own learning style, as well as that of the student.

As a parent, when you identify how your child learns best, you can help the child have more positive learning experiences in school. Understanding your child's learning style can help you communicate more effectively with him or her and assist in guiding the child through academic challenges. In addition to being aware of your child's strengths, it's equally important to help your child strengthen his or her weaker areas. The more you learn about your student's learning style, the easier it is to understand why some aspects of school are easy for them and other aspects are not.

The changing role of the classroom teacher

Today's classrooms are extremely diverse. Students possess a wide range of backgrounds, interests, experiences, abilities, and learning styles. Accommodating all of these differences is possibly the single greatest challenge for today's teachers.

To meet this challenge, teachers need a deep understanding and a strong desire to make content approachable for the diverse groups of students. Besides understanding the content, teachers must also have a solid understanding of their students. They must recognize and respect the importance of building strong relationships with each student.

Understanding learning styles means educators have a better understanding of how to offer students different options so learning activities can be tailored to each individual's preferred learning style(s). To be successful leaders, teachers must provide a variety of learning approaches for their students so these individual differences can be recognized and accommodated. Understanding the various ways in which children learn, as well as how they interact with and process information, can help educators modify their lessons so that all students have an equal opportunity for success. This knowledge is also beneficial for parents so they can be more supportive at home.

It is imperative that today's teachers be able to describe and identify learning styles. Students do not have a single learning style. The brain works in many different ways. We use many styles to learn, depending on the circumstances. Once teachers are able to identify various learning styles, they can use that information to develop instruction tailored to the particular styles represented in their classrooms and to manage their classroom according to these styles.

Knowing his or her learning style helps that student recognize his or her preferred method for taking in information. Furthermore, as multiple intelligence theory tells us, students will know how to express his or her "smartness" to the outside world.

Summary of learning styles discussed throughout the book

There has been a great deal of research on learning styles over the last 50 years. This book summarizes that research and provides applications for your classroom.

Chapter 1 describes the work of Anthony Gregorc. Gregorc's learning style research has helped teachers recognize how personality differences can either enhance or impede communication between individuals.

Chapter 2 focuses on the work of Dunn and Dunn. Their research identified significant stimuli that may influence learning and manipulate the school environment.

Chapter 3 discusses the work of Howard Gardner, who identified individual talents or aptitudes in his Multiple Intelligences theories.

Chapter 4 includes the work of Neil D. Fleming, who developed the VARK questionnaire to assess an indivdual's preferred means of receiving information and delivering communication.

This book discusses the work and research done by each of these leading researchers and the impact his or her work has had on classrooms around the world. In **Chapter 5**, we offer a description of how to use your knowledge of learning styles to design effective, individualized assessments based on the theories of each researcher.

Relationships exist among the researchers discussed throughout this book. Fleming and Gregorc both focus on perceptual modes of giving and receiving information. Dunn and Dunn focus on the effects of environmental stimuli on the efficiency of the perceptual mode, and Gardner's work reflects both the aspects of perceived preferences for gathering and processing information along with aspects of psychological partialities. Because the theories often overlap, **Chapter 6** shows how we were able to integrate all the research into an Individual Learning Plan (ILP) system called The Yes I Can! Model. Sample ILPs are discussed, and blank templates are provided in the Appendix so you can start designing your own Yes I Can! Model portfolios and assessments.

The **Appendix** also offers sample student surveys and feedback forms designed as tools for the teacher to use to reflect upon his or her own practice as to whether the strategies used in class were actually effective. A complete reference list is also provided, along with additional resources such as links to useful websites.

Chapter 1

Anthony Gregorc

Description

Dr. Anthony Gregorc determined that humans make sense of the world in various ways. The ways in which an individual gathers and interprets knowledge is unique to that individual. Dr. Gregorc's Mind Style research resulted in four different styles through which one perceives and interprets the world: Concrete Sequential (CS), Abstract Sequential (AS), Abstract Random (AR), and Concrete Random (CR).

Concrete and *abstract* describe the perceptual qualities that an individual uses to refer to the world in which he or she lives. Concrete individuals relate the world to their physical and active "self," while abstract thinkers focus on their feelings, relationships, and ideas. Concrete thinkers catalog information directly through the five senses: smell, sight, taste, touch, and hearing. Use of one's concrete ability involves dealing with present situations, understanding "it is what it is." Abstract thinkers visualize, imagine ideas, and understand or believe what one actually cannot see. An abstract thinker uses insight and imagination to understand that "things aren't always what they seem." Although most people possess both concrete and abstract perceptual abilities, each person is usually more comfortable using one quality over the other. For example, those whose natural strength is concrete may speak in a direct, no-nonsense manner, while one whose natural strength is the abstract may use more subtle ways to communicate.

There are two ordering abilities that go along with the perceptual qualities in Gregorc's learning style model: *sequential* and *random*. Sequential thinkers organize information in a linear, step-by-step manner. Sequential thinkers use logical trains of thought and traditional approaches to deal with information.

Sequential thinkers often have a plan to follow, rather than relying on impulse. Random thinkers allow their minds to organize information in chunks that occur in no particular order. Those using this random ability skip procedural steps but still accomplish the desired result. Random thinkers are more impulsive and impromptu in their actions. As with the perceptual qualities, each person has both ordering abilities, but usually displays one dominant preference.

Gregorc identified four types of learners but noted that no learning style is superior; each is simply different. Each style can be effective in its own way. The important thing is that individuals become more aware of which learning and thinking style works best for them. Once a person knows his or her own style, then it may become easier to analyze the learning styles of others. This understanding will help individuals understand each other better. It may also make people more flexible.

As mentioned earlier, there are four combinations of the strongest perceptual and ordering abilities for each individual: Concrete Sequential (CS), Abstract Random (AR), Abstract Sequential (AS), and Concrete Random (CR). Most individuals possess aspects of all combinations but favor one over the others. The chart on the following page summarizes these characteristics.

Gregorc's Mind Style characteristics

Concrete Sequential individuals	Concrete Random individuals
<ul><li>are natural organizers and closely follow directions.</li><li>prefer carrying out tasks step-by-step.</li><li>enjoy hands-on projects.</li><li>favor things to be ordered and arranged in specific ways.</li><li>have difficulty sitting still for long periods of time.</li><li>look for constructive activities to do.</li><li>need and enjoy structured situations.</li><li>prefer clear and definite directions.</li><li>have a fear of being wrong.</li></ul>	<ul><li>are extremely independent and competitive.</li><li>enjoy taking risks.</li><li>often skip details and steps.</li><li>are extremely curious.</li><li>seek innovation.</li><li>prefer investigation and experimentation.</li><li>exhibit originality and creativity.</li><li>dislike structure.</li><li>often fail to read instructions or directions.</li></ul>
Abstract Sequential individuals	**Abstract Random individuals**
<ul><li>think in structured, logical, and organized ways.</li><li>avidly read for new information and ideas presented in logical ways.</li><li>prefer quiet environments in which to think and work.</li><li>fear appearing foolish or uninformed.</li><li>seek intellectual recognition.</li><li>gather information and analyze ideas.</li><li>are lifelong learners.</li><li>enjoy debating controversial ideas.</li></ul>	<ul><li>have a fear of not being liked or approved of.</li><li>are highly imaginative.</li><li>tend to personalize information.</li><li>focuses on relationships and friendships.</li><li>tend to take on multiple projects or tasks at the same time.</li><li>enjoy learning through discussions and sharing of ideas.</li><li>dislike routines and order.</li><li>are very sensitive to feelings.</li><li>are flexible and respond to change easily.</li></ul>

History

Anthony Gregorc is recognized for his work with learning styles and the development of the Mind Styles Model™. His work with learning styles is of interest in the education field because it provides insight for educators to consider how the mind works in assisting students with achieving academic success. Over the course of many years, Gregorc has developed theories about learning styles and their effect on learning and education.

In the early 1970s, Gregorc was working on an assessment tool to address what, why, and how individuals learn. Gregorc's interpretation of style was based on his Mediation Ability Theory that describes how the mind works. His interest in learning style developed from his own experiences working in a variety of teacher-related jobs. Throughout Gregorc's career, he served as a teacher, administrator, and college professor. Gregorc taught both math and science. He has been principal of a laboratory school for gifted youth and an associate professor at two American universities. His personal and professional experiences in various educational settings led him to identify and examine the idea of individual differences. For Gregorc, the style reflected in one's behavior is an indication of the qualities of one's mind. His learning styles ideas are based on brain hemispherical research.

In 1982, Gregorc developed the Gregorc Style Delineator™ to assess a person's perceptual and ordering abilities. The Gregorc instrument is used by numerous educators to determine the mind styles of their students and to help students realize that individuals learn in different ways. As an example, the Gregorc instrument can be used to discuss cognitive learning preferences for each learning style. *Perceptual abilities* refer to the means by which individuals take in information, and *ordering abilities* refer to ways in which individuals organize the information. Perceptual abilities may be described in concrete or abstract terms. The qualities that control one's ordering abilities are *sequence* and *randomness*. All individuals possess all of these qualities, but the qualities are used in different ways depending on the individual.

Application of this model for everyday classroom use and lesson planning

Now that you have the background and history associated with Gregorc's Mind Styles characteristics, we can apply this knowledge to everyday classroom settings. If the Gregorc model is the modality of choice, then teachers must create lessons to meet the needs of the learners identified in the model. Because Gregorc does not believe in surveying students to identify learning style, his product brochures and website state that "no student instrument exists for technical, ethical, and philosophical reasons." He feels that labels may be too constricting. He has created a set of questions for adults called the Gregorc Style Delineator™ that can be purchased from his website at http://www.gregorc.com. Using the Gregorc Style Delineator™ to check personal learning styles, individuals read through 15 sets of words that are arranged in groups of four. They then choose two from each set that best describe them. These descriptors are then tallied and tabulated on a weighted scale to determine preferred ways of processing information. (Go to http://www.thelearningweb.net/personalthink.html for a personal thinking style survey based on the Gregorc Style Delineator™.)

Using the information from the following tables, teachers are encouraged to make close observations of their students early in the school year to identify the learning style characteristics exhibited by each one and then plan tailored lessons accordingly. Once teachers understand the diversity of their students' learning styles and the implications for their preferred methods of learning, they understand more clearly how to organize the instruction. Consistently using Gregorc's learning style terminology also affords the students a new educational identity that they may not have been previously aware of, especially in the specific terms of Concrete Sequential, Abstract Random, etc. Depending on the age of the students, they may already know how they learn best but probably are not aware of the specific terminology of Gregorc's labels.

The following tables include characteristics of each type of learner. Information on what each type of learner does best, the difficulties associated with each type of learner, tips for the instructional focus, the preferred learning focus, and details about the ideal learning environment are included in the table. This information can assist teachers in meeting the diverse needs of each type of learner.

Concrete Sequential learners

Characteristics	Preferred learning environments
• practical • organize • detailed • efficient	• orderly • quiet • routines to follow • highly structured
What is difficult for these learners?	**Instructional focus**
• working in groups • use of imagination • abstract ideas • incomplete or unclear directions • dealing with unpredictable people • working in unorganized environments • making choices • answering "what if" questions • dealing with opposing views	• working systematically, step-by-step • having a schedule to follow • a structured environment • routines, directions, and details • knowing what's expected of them • realistic situations
Preferred learning strategies	**What do these learners do best?**
• hands-on approaches • use of computers • projects • workbooks • gathering data • guided practice • whole-group instruction	• apply ideas in a practical way • fine-tune ideas to increase proficiency • follow directions • gather facts • work well within time limits

Student profile: Katie is a typical concrete sequential learner. She follows directions very well and is adept in following the routines and procedures the teacher has established. She isn't afraid to keep other students in line. Katie is attentive to details and is the go-to gal if you want to know what is going on in her classroom. She likes choices to be black or white and struggles with the gray areas. She is the "planner."

Abstract Sequential learners

Characteristics	Preferred learning environments
• critical • analytical • intellectual • theoretical	• orderly • quiet • routines to follow • highly structured
What is difficult for these learners? • working with those of differing views • lack of time for thorough work • repetitive tasks • specific rules and regulations • not being the center of conversation • expressing emotions • creative writing tasks • open-ended problems	**Instructional focus** • independent study • learning more by watching than doing • use of abstract ideas • exploring theory and concepts • applying reason and logic
Preferred learning strategies • lecture • reading • content mastery • conceptual problems • research • debates • textbooks • projects • ability grouping	**What do these learners do best?** • gather information prior to making a decision • analyze situations before acting • use facts to prove or disprove theories • solve problems • research information • work alone

Student profile: Lane is a typical abstract sequential learner. He enjoys working alone to solve problems. He believes he can do the task better than most, and he may be critical of other's opinions. Lane works best with traditional methods of instruction and yearns for respect of his intellectual abilities. He will be sure to analyze the situation prior to making a decision. Although he may be a quiet student, people listen to Lane when he talks. He is the "thinker."

Concrete Random learners

Characteristics	What do these learners do best?
• inspirational • inventive • risk-taking	• use insight to solve problems • use real world experience to learn • experiment to find answers • solve problems independently
What is difficult for these learners? • routines, restrictions, and limitations • keeping detailed records • having limited or no options • showing how they got the answer • formal reports • completing projects • prioritizing	**Instructional focus** • open-ended activities • investigations • experiments • multiple options • projects/activities • application over practical situations
Preferred learning strategies • brainstorming • games • simulations • experiments • problem solving	**Preferred learning environments** • self-directed • original and unique in nature • noisy, high-energy environments

Student profile: Eli is a concrete random learner. Eli finds new ways to solve old problems. He likes to take risks and thinks outside the box. Eli prefers learning from real-life experiences. Don't ask him for details, as Eli doesn't like to sweat the small stuff. He is the "free-spirit."

Abstract Random learners

Characteristics	What do these learners do best?
• flexible • emotional • imaginative • interpretative	• listen to others • develop positive relationships • understand feelings and emotions • enhance accord in group situations
What is difficult for these learners? • competition • concentrating on one thing at a time • working with unfriendly people • giving exact details • interacting with authoritarian figures • working individually • being corrected • working within time limits	**Instructional focus** • interpretation • explanation • peer-teaching • communication • illustration
Preferred learning strategies • group work • mapping • music • media • role playing	**Preferred learning environments** • noncompetitive atmosphere • personal attention • emotional support

Student profile: Susie is an abstract random learner. She is very flexible, works well with others, and likes it when everyone gets along. Susie communicates well and prefers working in groups to working by herself. Susie is the "social butterfly."

What can a teacher do with this information?

Start by sharing the different types of mind styles with students to introduce the terminology and to begin conversations about these learning styles. Observe the behavior of their students and administer the Gregorc Style Delineator™ as well, to acquire more information about how your students learn best. After administering the assessment, discuss the results with each student for clarification, verification, and possible modification. Personal conversations with students after a learning style inventory are crucial to clarify the results and to plant the seeds for working with those particular learning styles.

Then, start including various methods or strategies tailored to the four different mind styles in your instruction. Teachers can establish one learning objective and create four activity alternatives from which students can choose to reach that learning goal. For example, Abstract Sequential learners may choose to read a text or listen to an audiotape. Abstract Random learners may participate in discussion groups or watch a video. Concrete Sequential learners may take a field trip or complete computer-assisted instructional programs. Concrete Random learners might enact a simulated meeting or play a game.

Knowing how each student learns best is essential to effective classroom teaching. Students will welcome the attention they receive as an individual and also welcome a new educational identity. Administrators will also appreciate the efforts of the teacher to gain new insight on each individual student and to provide routine learning activities tailored to each student's learning styles.

Sample activities for each learning style

The setting:

High school students are reading the novel *The Adventures of Huckleberry Finn* (Twain 2004). Students will develop a better understanding of the novel, as well as the time period in American history in which it takes place by carrying out the following learning activities based on Gregorc's learning styles.

Activity #1: Raft Model

Learning style preference: Concrete Sequential

Description: The students design, research, and use appropriate materials to create a model of the raft used by Jim and Huck to float down the Mississippi River. Then, each student must type a short description of how the model was made, including why the materials used were chosen. Students work individually. The teacher provides a schedule for completion of tasks that also serves as a checklist for progress.

Accommodations for special needs populations:

English language learners: These students thrive when they are working independently on hands-on projects while receiving personal attention from the teacher. Producing a physical model of the raft will eliminate common language barriers, as well.

Above-level learners: Students' descriptions should include illustrations and at least three research sources used to help them design their rafts.

Below-level learners: Allow them more time to design their model with fewer requirements for the length of the description. The teacher should provide a schedule for students to follow that includes daily expectations for progress.

Varying instructional methods according to grade level:

Elementary level: Teachers may read this book or a similar book to their students. A suggested project is to build rafts out of craft sticks. Students follow step-by-step instructions to create the raft, which also serves as a good lesson in reading directions.

Intermediate level: For middle school students, hold a competition to determine which raft floats the best.

Secondary level: Students research practical designs for their rafts and incorporate knowledge from other disciplines, such as physics principles of buoyancy and density, into their descriptions. Students present their models and justify the design and the materials they selected.

Activity #2: Two-Sided Debate

Learning style preference: Abstract Sequential

Description: Students debate Huck's decision to help Jim escape from slavery. Students must organize the facts, including three main points to support their opinions. Students can conduct independent research to gather information prior to the debate.

Accommodations for special needs populations:

English language learners: Allow these students to work with those more proficient in the language. They can use index cards with the information they gathered. Assist these students in paraphrasing and breaking down difficult concepts prior to the debate.

Above-level learners: Students can gather additional information to support their argument prior to the debate. They may manage the publicity and advertising for the event and videotape it for later critique.

Below-level learners: These students should be active participants in the debate but may need assistance gathering unique facts and ideas that will support their opinion. Added attention will encourage below-level students to participate and feel like viable members of the team.

Varying instructional methods according to grade level:

Elementary level: Read the selection to elementary students and discuss students' opinions about Huck's decision to help Jim escape from slavery. This could take place through lessons on social studies or on personal responsibility.

Intermediate level: Students will debate their own opinions on this issue. The teacher may lead the debate process while students choose the side they wish to argue.

Secondary level: These students can carry out a full-blown, organized debate. Invite an audience to critique the debate and provide feedback.

··

Activity #3: Newspaper Editorial

Learning style preference: Concrete Random

Description: Students write an editorial stating whether they recommend reading *The Adventures of Huckleberry Finn*. Students must back up their statements with strong reasoning. They may conduct brainstorming sessions with peers, parents, or community members to gather information for their editorials.

Accommodations for special needs populations:

English language learners: Students will choose how to present their editorial. They may feel more comfortable writing their thoughts rather than voicing their opinions. Encourage them to work with others who are proficient in speaking and writing the language.

Above-level learners: Students can produce podcast editorials that challenges them to incorporate the use of advanced technologies.

Below-level learners: These students need ample time to create their editorials. Encourage brainstorming sessions with the whole group so these students can glean ideas from their peers.

Varying instructional methods according to grade level:

Elementary level: Students can create their own illustrated or computer generated covers for *The Adventures of Huckleberry Finn* (2004).

Intermediate level: Students can write editorials for their own school newspaper. Encourage them to brainstorm with their peers prior to writing the editorials.

Secondary level: Require students to provide support in the form of modern-day analogies. Students can conduct brainstorming sessions with peers, parents, community members, and others to gather information from the internet or news sources.

······································

Activity #4: Monologue

Learning style preference: Abstract Random

Description: Students choose a character from the novel and write a two-minute monologue that portrays a character's feelings about an event from the novel. Students must record the point at which the monologue takes place and understand the content of the monologue. Students may work in groups to practice their monologue presentations. They may also add music, video footage, or background effects.

Accommodations for special needs populations:

English language learners: Students may design the props or background sets for these monologues that evoke the mood or reflect the tone of the events. Many times, these learners are highly artistic and enjoy showing off their creative talents.

Above-level learners: Allow students to assist with organizing the presentations of these monologues, including creating a program, arranging for an audience, or writing a review.

Below-level learners: Students can create visuals or use tableau poses to help depict their monologues. These presentations can be shorter than those required for above-level students.

Varying instructional methods according to grade level:

Elementary level: Elementary students enjoy playacting roles based on particular characters from books that are read to them.

Intermediate level: This student enjoys working with his or her peer group to produce presentations. Adding music and video footage also appeals to this grade level.

Secondary level: These students should be required to add music and video footage to their presentations. Their presentations may also be videotaped for class viewing.

Teachers and parents working together to accommodate these learning styles

Parents and teachers must work with the student to design activities, access resources, and develop learning guidelines that will provide the student the best chance for success in accomplishing his or her learning goals. As a parent, speak with your child's teacher if you have questions or feel his or her learning style strengths are not being addressed in the classroom. Parents who are aware of how their child learns best and can show them how to best help themselves will help ensure academic success.

Teachers should encourage parents to ask questions instead of offering constructive criticism of the child's work.

Parents and caregivers are key players in ensuring a student's academic success. Knowing how a child learns best and supporting the child in this learning style will improve learning and increase success in all academic areas.

How to offer home support

Concrete Sequential learners	Abstract Sequential learners
• Arrange a study corner at home. This area needs to be quiet and free from the television, radio, and other people. • Let the child study for several short periods of time, rather than one long period of time. • Show the child how to make outlines of information prior to writing essays. • Offer lots of specific and positive feedback.	• Provide a study corner for a consistent work area. • Provide a relatively quiet area, with possibly the addition of soft background music. • Have students use highlighters to mark important parts of their notes to encourage them to reread information. • Provide constructive feedback.
Concrete Random learners	**Abstract Random learners**
• Allow students to work in atmospheres that are lively, noisy, and interesting. • Encourage these learners to make webs of key ideas, along with visual and verbal associations. • Because they enjoy solving problems their own way, allow them to use hands-on explanations. • Challenge these learners to meet time goals as additional incentives to learning.	• Resolve emotional dilemmas before homework time. • Provide a means for creating illustrations of concepts to enhance learning. • Let them work with a study-buddy or be surrounded by others at a library. • Ask leading questions to help them discover where they can improve instead of criticizing their work (e.g., "What are some examples you could give?" versus "You didn't give enough details.")

Conclusion

The reading lesson in Ms. Carol's second grade involves cause and effect. The teacher reads *Tops and Bottoms* (Stevens 1995) and *The Runaway Bunny* (Brown and Hurd 2005) to the class. As a class, they discuss cause and effect in both stories. Next, the students will attend various centers to learn more about cause and effect. The teacher assigns centers according to Gregorc's learning style characteristics.

At Learning Center One, students will work individually to complete cause and effect reading comprehension questions and play the Cause-and-Effect Matching game. Ms. Carol ensures that the directions are clear and presented in a step-by-step manner. She will give these students a time limit to accomplish the activities.

At Learning Center Two, students have a choice of activities. They may choose to play the Cause and Effect Matching Game in a group of two to four students or work with two or three other students to develop a play that has examples of cause and effect. Students at this center are self-directed and easily come up with original ideas for their play. This center is a high-energy, somewhat noisy environment, so the teacher must position the center so that the noise does not disturb others.

At Learning Center Three, students will also work individually. They will watch the video *Chicken Little* and write a summary of the story that includes five cause-and-effect examples. They will also write an alternative ending to the story that includes cause-and-effect situations. Allow these students as much time as needed to complete their assigned tasks.

At Learning Center Four, students will work cooperatively to make a poster with five pictures and write the cause and effect under the picture. Students may draw the picture or cut it from a magazine. The teacher must provide Learning Center Four with plenty of personal attention.

Think about it!

1. Which center is tailored for Concrete Sequential learners? Abstract Sequential? Concrete Random? Abstract Random?

2. Would you prefer all students to rotate through all centers or match students with centers according to their learning style strengths?

3. How did the teacher both differentiate and tailor her instruction according to Gregorc's learning styles?

4. How would you communicate the purpose of such centers to your administrators, colleagues, and parents?

Chapter 2

Dunn and Dunn Learning Styles Model

Description

This model is quite possibly the most widely used and researched learning-styles model in the history of American education. The Dunn and Dunn Learning Styles Model is the outcome of research initiated by the New York State Department of Education, in collaboration with the National Association of Secondary School Principals (NASSP) (1978).

Dr. Rita Dunn, a former professor of Innovative Administrative Leadership and Teaching Young Children to Read at St. John's University, New York, was one of the first scholars to study the learning styles concept. She found that there was a very strong research base for learning styles and urged all educators to work with them. Sadly, Rita Dunn passed away in 2009.

The Dunn and Dunn Learning Styles Model, established by Rita and her husband Kenneth in 1977, was one of the first models to emphasize identifying a student's learning style through a diagnostic inventory. Their work continues today at St. John's University in Queens, New York at the Center of the Study of Learning and Teaching Styles.

In addition, there is still a large focus on consistent teacher training throughout the national and international sites where the model is taught, practiced, and evaluated. For the model to be successful, the teachers are trained to adopt the underlying principles as their own and must commit to them to continue the training.

This model uniquely pairs educational dogma, curricular strategies, and diagnostic tools with a view of the whole child by using techniques that address what the teacher does, what the student does, how the classroom is organized, the procedures and materials to be used, etc. As teachers become more familiar with the model, they can identify the knowledge and skills that they themselves need in order to perform at the mastery level.

The Dunn and Dunn model is organized into four basic components:

- the principles of the model
- learning style dimensions
- learning style diagnostics
- impact on the classroom

History

For over 40 years, Kenneth and Rita Dunn were leaders in establishing a learning styles revolution in education. Rita, who was a professor and coordinator of St. John's University's Instructional Leadership Doctoral Program, was the first full-time female professor in the School of Education in 1976. In 1979, she became director of the Center for the Study of Learning and Teaching Styles.

She received St. John's University's first Outstanding Faculty Achievement Gold Medal in May of 1986 and its first Award for Excellence in Graduate Teaching in 1995. Dr. Dunn authored many books, book chapters, research monographs, and articles. She received many awards for her scholarship and teaching and was recognized around the world as a leader among educators.

Kenneth Dunn currently works as a professor and coordinates the Educational Leadership Program at Queens College in New York. However, he first earned his stripes working in the trenches as a superintendent in several districts throughout New York and New Jersey, and had much success along the way with his focus on collaborative leadership. Many of Dr. Dunn's writings have been cited in a fleet of prominent texts by influential educational leaders. Once his work even landed a reference in the popular publication, *Redbook* (1982) in an article about understanding learning styles for parents and their children by A. L. Ball.

In 1987, Rita and Kenneth shared an induction into the Hunter College Hall of Fame, another shining example of their successful collaboration.

Starting in 1967, Drs. Rita and Kenneth Dunn compiled and analyzed educational research concerned with how people learn. They accumulated an abundance of research, dating as far back as 80 years, that repeatedly validated the individual differences in how each student begins to concentrate on, sort, grasp, and retain new and complicated information.

Initially, in 1972, the Dunns identified 12 variables that drastically differentiated students. Three years later, they reported 18 variables. By 1979, they had integrated hemispheric preference and global/analytic inclinations into their classifications.

Since 1989, research conducted by the Dunns, their colleagues, doctoral students, graduate professors, and researchers has confirmed that when students are instructed based on their identified learning-style preferences, they show statistically increased academic success, an improved attitude toward instruction, and better self-control than if they are taught without attention to their preferred styles.

These findings were recorded in the *Synthesis of the Dunn and Dunn Learning-Style Model Research* in 2003 by Rita Dunn and Shirley A. Griggs of St. John's University:

- While teachers believed in individualized practice, their belief was not reflected in their actual practice (Mawhinney 2002).
- Since the turn of the 19th century, assessments have been used to compare teaching practices with academic success, suggesting that teachers should attempt to match their teaching style to each student's learning style.

- When the use of learning styles is promoted by a school's administration, dramatic academic gains occur (Dunn and DeBello 1999; Dunn and Griggs 1988). The most significant differences in student achievement come from teacher expertise and certifications (Armour-Thomas, Clay, Domanico, Bruno, and Allen 1989; Ferguson 1991; Sanders and Horn 1998).

This information is both refreshing and unsettling. On one hand, teachers easily accept that children differ with various strengths and weaknesses. On the other hand, they fail to align their everyday teaching to this belief. The principle that all students learn differently must be believed mutually among the faculty if a schoolwide change for serving the individual preferences of students is to be plausible, much less successful. The cohesive agreement among educators will serve as a foundation for the change in culture that will naturally occur schoolwide if *every* educator sees the value in differentiating by learning style.

According to this research, this idea is widely accepted. However, educators are often hampered by over-burdened schedules; oversized classrooms with inadequate resources, equipment, paraprofessionals and specialists; insufficient mentoring of new teaching professionals; and a lack of support in disciplinary issues.

Administrators interested in useful in-house professional development that will have a large impact on student achievement should encourage teachers to collaborate, even if that means creating a more supportive schedule. Teachers need to share ideas and to discuss students as individuals with different strengths and needs that require different "prescriptions" for learning. Educators are in desperate need for time to digest and reflect on the mass of triangulated data that accompanies mandated testing and accountability and takes up much class time. In addition, discussions between teachers would allow for interdisciplinary curricular alignment and interdependent relationships among professionals of all specialties and content areas.

Application of this model for everyday classroom use and lesson planning

Dunn and Dunn's model principles

Teachers trained in the Dunn and Dunn model must inherently believe that most individuals are capable of learning and that all learners have strengths even if they differ from each other. Recognizing that these instructional preferences exist is the first step to restructuring teaching methods and student activities. Teachers must be aware that the learning environment and available resources can enhance the response of students with various learning styles.

Familiarity with learning styles is a key determining factor for designing learning and instruction in the classroom. If the students are in an environment where they can be responsive and active contributors and where the environment is well matched to their preferred method of learning, then they will statistically attain higher levels of achievement. Students can then be armed with knowledge of their own strengths to learn new material, even in different classrooms (Dunn and Dunn 1993).

Dunn and Dunn's learning style dimensions

The "dimensions" within this model are layers of stimuli that affect the learning process and go beyond simply categorizing a learner as visual, auditory, and so on. Unlike the Gregorc, Gardner, and VARK models—where diagnostics take into account only one dimension of learning—the Dunn and Dunn model involves five dimensions, each broken down into various elements of stimuli preferences.

These dimensions consider the environmental needs of the learner and help the teacher make simple changes in the classroom based on the majority of their learners' needs. The five main classifications of stimuli preferences are as follows: environmental, emotional, sociological, physiological, and psychological.

Each of these stimuli preferences are worth reviewing for any classroom teacher. However, to implement every preference for all students requires extensive training in this model.

In considering these preferences, it would be maddening to try to meet the needs of each individual learner for every hour of every day and to change instruction depending upon the learning activity taking place. However, if these preferences are considered for enhancing learning on a general basis for the classroom, then the model should be beneficial.

Environmental stimuli include preferences for:

Sound	<ul><li>This refers to a student's preference for or need of background music while learning.</li><li>Some students prefer hearing music for the whole class during individualized activities; others prefer to have more control over volume, sound choice, etc., using their own multimedia devices.</li></ul>
Light	<ul><li>This refers to the type of light (natural versus synthetic), as well as the level of light (soft, dim, bright, etc.) available in the classroom. Obviously, lighting may change to enhance the performance of LCD projectors or interactive screens. However, students may indicate their preferred levels and types of light during individual work, classroom discussions, and quiet reading times.</li></ul>
Temperature	<ul><li>Temperature may vary depending on the type of activity involved. During tactile or kinesthetic activities, cooler temperatures may be preferred, while warmer temperatures may be more appropriate for individual study.</li><li>Many teachers do not have control over the temperature in their classrooms. Keeping a window open or using a portable fan may be an option with permission from an administrator.</li></ul>
Design	<ul><li>Where is the teacher's desk?</li><li>Where are the student desks? Or are there couches, pillows on the floor, and recliners instead?</li><li>Where do you spend most of your instructional time, and where is that in relationship to the door, windows, etc., which could be possible distractions to instruction?</li><li>Ask for student suggestions about organizing classroom furniture so it can be most comfortable for them and suitable for you.</li></ul>

Emotional stimuli include preferences for:

Motivation	• Motivation includes the source and extent of interest a student has in learning. • Some students are intrinsically self-motivated (some by specific topics and some by the level of contact they may have with their peers), and others need extrinsic motivation in the form of adult feedback and external reward systems. In addition, a learner may be motivated by more than one of these factors at a time, such as a reward offered by parents in addition to an intrinsic interest in the topic being studied. • Though the topic of extrinsic motivation may be widely debated among educators, simply understanding what motivates your students can play a key role in helping them meet classroom expectations.
Persistence	• Persistence refers to a student's attention span, his or her ability to do the task, his or her interest in the task, the mode of completing the task, and the level of appropriateness for the task assigned. • Some students prefer to work on one task at a time, while others are comfortable performing a variety of tasks at once.
Responsibility	• Responsibility refers to the level of accountability, supervision, guidance, and feedback that a learner prefers while working. • Some learners are capable of doing assignments on their own and prefer the freedom of checking in with you periodically; others want frequent feedback and need more supervision from you to ensure that they stay on task.
Structure	• Structure includes delivery of instruction and whether students receive a complete explanation before beginning work or are allowed to attempt the assignment in his or her own way. • A student who enjoys structure may want clearly stated objectives, a timeline, and a list of acceptable resources. Be sure to establish a rapport with these students so their individual creativity can still come through in an assignment. • A student who does not want or need so much structure may prefer a range of choices for demonstrating mastery of objectives. Allow these students to choose a check-in time with you for feedback, and be prepared to offer some latitude in the timeline for completion.

Sociological stimuli include preferences for:

Working alone	• Learners with this preference want to figure out a task on their own. This preference may be situational, or it may depend on the type of task involved. • Some learners prefer to learn to do a task on their own but then want to work with someone else.
Working in pairs	• These learners prefer to work with one other person instead of a group.
Working with peers and teams	• These students prefer to work in small groups with high interaction levels and to complete the task as a team.
Working with an adult	• When working with an authority figure, some students lean heavily on adults for guidance while others may react negatively and feel defensive even at the mere presence of an adult, despite the adult's best intentions.
A variety of situations	• Students reach different levels of involvement in a variety of tasks. • Some students value procedures and routine patterns, while others prefer a range of activities while learning.

Physiological stimuli include preferences of:

Perception	• This describes how a student uses his or her sensory abilities to retain information. • Some students may prefer audiotapes, CDs, music, podcasts, and videos to help them learn new information. • Other learners may prefer visual materials such as pictures, posters, flowcharts, maps, and reading. • For tactile or kinesthetic learners, building a model, doing a science project, keeping a diary, or writing a storybook may be the way they best preserve information.
Intake	• This element deals with the need to have drinks or food while involved in learning activities. • Food and drink are too often frowned upon in the classroom but can be highly beneficial to learning retention. If a student is hungry, he or she is not able to think about much else. • Some teachers find it highly beneficial to offer a snack time during midmorning or to allow students to bring in snacks for the class on a rotational basis.
Time	• Energy levels vary during different times of the day. • Do tasks that require a great deal of concentration during the early part of the day. Schedule more kinesthetic tasks for the afternoon.
Mobility	• This refers to students who need to move their body, even unconsciously, while involved in a learning activity. • Some students are able to sit still for long periods of time, especially if the topic is engaging. However, a teacher may find great success by allowing or incorporating simple movements (such as walking, standing, jumping, etc.) into everyday learning activities for those who learn better when given some freedom to move.

Psychological stimuli include preferences of:

Global/analytical	• A student with a global learning preference needs to see the "big picture" and an overview of its relevance before diving into the details of the topic. • Students with a more analytical approach find value in the sequence of learning one detail at a time so that they can complete the activity by putting the parts together to make the "big picture."
Hemisphericity	• The dominant side of the brain is an indicator of some specific preferences. • Left-brained dominant individuals tend to be more analytical and are partial to sequentially organized activity. • Right-brained dominant individuals tend to be more artistic, creative, and concerned with the topic as a whole.
Impulsive/reflective	• The time between considering information and using that information to make decisions varies between individuals. • Some students prefer to draw conclusions and make choices quickly, while others take their time to thoroughly think through all information before making a decision.

Using the charts on pages 41–45 as a reference, determine the answers to the following scenarios:

1. A student walks into your room listening to her iPod® and moves past you to a window seat at the back of the room. What has she already told you about her environmental preferences?

2. Kate and Jacob have been randomly assigned as partners for a project in your class. They were very glad to be partnered up at first because both are very creative students. While you were giving instructions, Kate was highlighting important items to remember and listening attentively. Jacob was writing down ideas for the project and waiting somewhat impatiently for you to finish so that he could get started. Once all pairs were working, Kate was reviewing the details of the instructions given

for the project, and Jacob jumped into finding information for the project. They began to argue about how to best begin and proceed through the rest of the class period. What are the preferred psychological and emotional stimuli differences of these two students? What challenges will this team face as they continue in the project? How would you approach this team to help them understand how each operates so they can reach a satisfactory level of teamwork? What could be the strengths of this pairing?

Dunn and Dunn's learning style diagnostics

The first Dunn and Dunn learning style diagnostic tests were developed in 1976 and have expanded into five different diagnostics based on age level over the last four decades:

1. The adult diagnostic (ages 17 and older) called "Building Excellence" (BE) was established in 1996.

2. The "Learning Styles: Clue to You!" (LSCY) diagnostic for middle school students (ages 10–13) was developed in 1998.

3. The "Learning in Vogue: Elements of Style" (LIVES) was designed for high school students (ages 14–18) in 2007.

4. The "Elementary Learning Styles Assessment" (ELSA) was created for elementary school students (ages 7–9) in 2007.

5. The "Observational Primary Assessment of Learning Styles" (OPALS) was designed for preschoolers and children in the primary grades (ages 3–6) in 2006.

All of these instruments are in multiple languages and have been used nationally and internationally. For more information on ordering specific diagnostics for your students, go to http://www.learningstyles.net.

This link also offers more details about each of these assessments. Most assessments cost $5.00 each and, depending on the age group, include a variety of questions from the five learning style dimensions: environmental, emotional, sociological, physiological, and psychological.

These assessments can be done online easily within a one-hour class period. Some of the tests include imagery, poetry, and humor to engage students in the assessment and to gain thorough insight as to the individual's preferences. The diagnostic creates a one-page profile accompanied by a full narrative explanation for interpreting the results.

There are tip sheets for the student, letters for the parents to help explain how the assessment results will be useful, and ways to create group profiles.

Simply reading this information and observing students to classify their preferences is both inefficient and inaccurate to assess your students. While observation alone may inspire you to teach in a more individualized manner, it is highly recommended that the assessment tools provided by Dunn and Dunn are used for the actual diagnosis of students' preferences.

What can a teacher do with this information?

While exploring the Dunn and Dunn model, teachers must carefully study the five basic dimensions that are explained in this chapter. The Dunn and Dunn model should not be executed without proper certification from a Dunn and Dunn training facility. However, the tables on pages 41–45 offer many ideas for teachers who wish to explore the model.

Some may find it overwhelming to try to meet all the different preferences for each learner. In an elementary classroom, spend more time with a few individual students throughout the day, and with those same few students all week. Depending upon the type of activity being done, you may be able to tailor learning preferences for your class a bit more easily than could a high school teacher working with a hundred and fifty students split between block-scheduled classes.

Experiment with changing a few environmental elements such as light, sound, and design, and then ask the students for feedback on those changes. You may find that your students are much more comfortable and prefer those changes to the standard classroom setup you inherited from a two-hundred-year-old educational system.

For example, you could add beanbag chairs, plants, and drapes to the room, allow iPods® or CD players during individual work time, or provide space for individual versus paired versus team learning environments throughout your classroom. You may get some extremely beneficial results and positive feedback from your students in the process.

You are in a sense "killing two birds with one stone" and may engage a larger number of your learners right from the start before you even begin to consider how their individual learning preferences can be applied to local, state, and national testing accommodations, tutoring opportunities, or use for course placement information.

As you read through the five different dimensions and the elements within each dimension, you probably identified very simple, inexpensive ways that you can change your classroom design and culture to better fit your students. Remember, the key advantage to all of this information is to create a learning atmosphere that is best for each individual student's ability to receive, apply, and retain the information presented in your classroom. Some examples of possible activities that utilize some preferences referred to in each of the five dimensions are described on pages 50–58.

Sample activities for each learning style

The setting:

Middle school science students have been studying the basics of Newton's Three Laws of Motion, in addition to the physics concepts of force and gravity. The activities on the following pages reinforce these concepts and emphasize specific preferences within the five main stimuli.

Activity #1: Spaghetti or Straw Towers

Learning preferences: This activity involves the following stimuli preferences:

• Environmental stimuli	cooler temperature due to kinesthetic activity
• Emotional stimuli	structure and responsibility
• Sociological stimuli	peers and teams
• Physiological stimuli	perceptual
• Psychological stimuli	global/analytical (preferably each team would include learners of both types)

Description: In this activity, students will assume different roles in the planning and design of a freestanding structure built with limited materials and within a certain amount of time. This activity may incorporate metric measurement of the tower; planning, designing, and building of a structure; a cost analysis; and graphing of class results. Within certain time frames (five minutes for planning, 10 minutes for building), students in teams of four will use limited materials to build the tallest freestanding structure. Student roles may include timer, materials manager, construction leader, and/or team captain. Sample materials for building may include scissors, 0.50 meters of masking tape, straws, one sheet of paper, spaghetti, small and large marshmallows, raisins, etc.

Accommodations for special needs populations:

English language learners: The use of symbols on index cards to aid in the job descriptions and roles for each student can be helpful. In addition, a short video condensed to highlight the major tasks involved in this activity (planning, building, and completion of the tower) may be useful for all students. For culminating activities, pair these learners with English language proficient students.

Above-level students: These students can analyze different aspects of data from their tower and then compare it to other towers in the classroom. Data analyses may include the most cost-effective tower, the tallest tower, the longest-standing structure, the structure that can hold the most number of pennies, etc. In addition, challenge these students to apply all three of Newton's laws to the tower.

Below-level learners: The hands-on portion of this activity will be beneficial to these students. For data analysis, have them focus on one set of data—such as height—and then compare the heights of all the towers in the room. They might also report on how one of Newton's Three Laws applies to the tower. In this way, they are able to analyze data and apply it but can focus on just one aspect, instead of all aspects of the tower at once.

Varying instructional methods according to grade level:

Elementary level: Offer step-by-step instructions for building a tower and then give students freedom to build a tower within a time limit. Have a class discussion on the pros and cons of each student's tower. In addition, elementary students could find pictures of their favorite buildings or structures and note similarities between those structures and the ones that they built. They could also apply Newton's laws by drawing arrows on the pictures to show the direction that forces—such as the weight of people, gravity, and the Earth pushing back—are exerting on the tower.

Intermediate level: This activity is most appropriate for middle school students. Challenge these students to analyze different aspects of the data from their tower and then compare it to other towers in the classroom. Data analyses may include the most cost-effective tower, the tallest tower, the longest-standing structure, the structure that can hold the most number of pennies, etc.

Secondary level: In addition to the data-analysis options mentioned above, high school students could compare the effectiveness of different portions of each tower by discussing any improvements that could be made. They should also incorporate the calculations, formulas, and units associated with the quantities involved (such as force, acceleration, mass, gravity, etc.). These students could also research and do presentations on the following topics: famous structures and the strongest shapes used in architecture; architectural and engineering disasters in history; a comparison of the steps an engineer takes and the steps student's took in the classroom when building a straw tower; and a cost comparison of the straw towers and the materials used in real buildings.

Activity #2: Newton's Biography

Learning preferences: This activity involves the following stimuli preferences:

• Environmental stimuli	moderate to warm temperatures
• Emotional stimuli	structure and persistence
• Sociological stimuli	self or pairs
• Physiological stimuli	perceptual
• Psychological stimuli	all types

Description: Students will make a *Microsoft PowerPoint®* presentation about significant events in Sir Isaac Newton's life by using the letters of the alphabet (one per slide) to describe that event. For example, slide #1 may be about an event that happened in Newton's life that begins with the letter *A*.

Accommodations for special needs populations:

English language learners: Provide guidance as they research Newton's life and include a video segment or DVD of Newton's life, with the Captions setting turned "on" to assist them in their research. Furthermore, by applying the alphabet to the significant events in Newton's life, this project is excellent for building vocabulary in a unique way. (Search for Isaac Newton at sites such as http://www.history.com or http://science.discovery.com.)

Above-level learners: Ask them to order the events chronologically while staying in sequence with the alphabet. In addition, have them import graphics, songs, and/or short movie clips into their *Microsoft PowerPoint®* presentations.

Below-level learners: These students will benefit from a brainstorming session to generate ideas before starting the project and modeling how to design a slide showcasing the letter of the alphabet represented on that slide. They can describe the information in their own words, include a citation if applicable, and tell how to import a picture to the slide. Below-level students will benefit greatly from seeing an example and working within a group first. In addition, provide all students the choice to work in partners on this project so these students will not feel singled out. By working with partners, they are more likely to be comfortable in completing both the research and *Microsoft PowerPoint,*® yet they may still require extra time for project completion.

Varying instructional methods according to grade level:

Elementary level: Elementary students may lack the computer skills and attention span to complete such a large task and may benefit from being assigned one letter of the alphabet. They can focus on designing one slide, and then the teacher can compile each slide into one presentation from the class on Sir Isaac Newton.

Intermediate level: This activity is adequate for the middle school learner but works best if done with partners. They can learn new skills in *Microsoft PowerPoint*® using tools such as animations, colors, and pattern variations on their slides. In addition, challenge the pairs to see how many different events in Newton's life they can find. As presentations are made, the pairs can tally how many facts were distinctive to only their *Microsoft PowerPoint*® presentations.

Secondary level: These students will enjoy both the challenge of learning to use new tools within this technology and in finding diverse facts about Newton. However, challenge them further by asking them to include five different ways that Newton's findings changed the world and/or are applied to the world today.

Activity #3: Newton's Laws Stations

Learning preferences: This activity involves a variety of stimuli preferences for each dimension.

• Environmental stimuli	moderate to warm temperatures
• Emotional stimuli	structure and persistence
• Sociological stimuli	self or pairs
• Physiological stimuli	perceptual
• Psychological stimuli	all types

Description: Students will travel around the classroom to participate in stations that suit them best. Out of eight possible stations, they must 1) complete activities in at least five of them and 2) use each of the Laws of Motion at some point. The purpose of the activities is for students to practice vocabulary, demonstrate understanding of concepts involved in Newton's Laws, and to investigate the life of Newton. The stimuli preferences offered at each station apply to a variety of learners and to every preference in each of the five dimensions at some point by maintaining a general approach to preferences for certain activities. This allows the teacher to appeal to each learner's preferences in a realistic and manageable way. For stations with online work, offer a one-to-one ratio by limiting the number of students at each station, making headphones and comfortable seating available, and providing dim lighting. For stations using hands-on activities, provide bright light, cooler temperatures with fans if possible, and plenty of choices for objects, colors, media, etc., to be used in their creations.

Station	Activity
Station #1 (Individual)	All About Newton: Students watch a video segment and answer questions.
Station #2 (Individual/ Pairs)	Newton's Laws Poster: Students draw a picture of an everyday activity for one of Newton's Laws (this law must be different from ones used in previous stations).

Station	Activity (cont.)
Station #3 (Individual/ Pairs)	Newton's Law Demo: Using a box of random objects, students create a demonstration of one of Newton's Laws (this law must be different from ones used in previous stations) and present it to another student or pair of students who then try to guess which law is being demonstrated.
Station #4 (Pairs)	Balloon Game: Using three different balloons (filled with air, water, and foam packing peanuts), students describe the forces exerted on each balloon.
Station #5 (Individual)	Basketball Drop: Using a tennis ball, basketball, and table-tennis ball, students place the tennis ball on top of the basketball and drop the pair from a set height. Then students describe what happened in terms of each of Newton's Laws. Students repeat the procedure, using different combinations of balls and recording their observations.
Station #6 (Individual)	Poem on a Palm®: Using a Palm® handheld device, students write a four-line poem that describes one of Newton's laws (this law must be different from ones used in previous stations).
Station #7 (Individual/ Pairs)	Clue Collection: Students review the questions that have already been put into the boxes on the table (the 300 box, 200 box, 100 box, and so on). Using an index card, students write a new question about one of Newton's Laws. Then they sort the questions into *Jeopardy!*® categories (100s, 200s, 300s, etc.) according to difficulty. Students write their initials on the bottom-right corner of each card.
Station #8 (Individual/ Pairs)	Gravity Guess: Students use a scale to determine their weight in pounds on Earth. Using mathematics, students convert their weight to kilograms and then calculate their weight in Newtons on Earth, Mars, and the moon.

Accommodations for special needs populations

English language learners: This activity requires students to be fairly independent from the teacher during the investigations at each station. Ways to make this activity more approachable for ELLs include pairing these students with strong partners for the stations; demonstrating the activity to be done at each station before having students attempt them; or discussing the complexity level of each station so that these students can choose those with which they feel most comfortable. In addition, post both a statement of each of Newton's Laws, as well as a picture of an example of each law for reference as students move through the stations.

Above-level learners: Adjust the level of questioning at each station, instruct them to complete the five stations required, and then encourage them to develop three *new* examples or ways to demonstrate each of the laws for the class. For an additional challenge activity, ask them to calculate where to place a marble so it will roll down a ramp and stop at a predetermined target.

Below-level learners: These students will need more supervision and help while moving through the stations. Try to "guide on the side" and ask questions of them as they move from one station to the next to determine if they are grasping the concepts. These students will also benefit from a review of each station afterward in whole-group or small-group discussion.

Varying instructional methods according to grade level:

Elementary level: Show the whole class a video about Newton's life, and decrease the number of stations to four or five. The more kinesthetic the stations, the more interest and motivation you will get from these students. For Station #2, display pictures cut from magazines and ask them to match the picture to one of Newton's laws. If needed, Station #3 and Stations #6–#8 can be adapted for whole-group instruction.

Intermediate level: As an extension activity, ask them to find their own everyday examples of applications of Newton's Laws. These students could also create a courtroom skit that determines whether a law of motion is being broken or is kept by viewing in-class demonstrations, video clips of cartoons, or pictures that have been drawn by students. Students can make their judgments and then defend their positions.

Secondary level: The high school students can create each of these stations. It is good practice for them to review the concepts, and through their creations, the teacher can see how well they understand each law. They create their own video of Newton's life, make their own flashcard games and quizzes, etc. Another way to determine if these students understand differences in the three laws is to have them develop and conduct their own open-ended lab during which they apply all three laws.

Teachers and parents working together to accommodate these learning styles

A common question for educators at parent-teacher conferences, especially from concerned parents, is "What can we do at home to help?" Unfortunately, although they are experts within their classrooms, most teachers do not feel comfortable and are ill-equipped outside of their own observations to give advice for learners on the home front. However, a teacher's personal, individualized understanding of a learner's preferences can guide this conversation more easily.

When engaging in a conversation about learning style preferences, try to remember that, for most parents, this type of individualized instruction was not a part of their own educational experiences. Avoid the use of educational jargon and explain the aspects of differentiation in your classroom as simply as possible. As their child's teacher, be prepared to engage in a conversation about the importance and advantages of using learning style preferences both at home and in school.

Share the preference diagnostic with the parents and explain what their student's preferences are for learning. Then share examples of how you are addressing their student's needs and preferences within your own classroom. Most parents will be grateful to have a teacher show such a personalized interest in their children, one that goes beyond the grading scale. It will also be helpful to share the information provided by the Dunn and Dunn assessments to guide their learner's progress at home. For example, if you are talking to the parents of a student who prefers low lighting, music, and cooler temperatures and who absorbs information better at night, suggest to parents to rearrange the child's bedroom or location of study in the house, dinnertime, and sleep schedule around his or her needs.

During a discussion with parents, keep in mind that each parent has his or her own learning style that may complement, conflict with, or be similar to the other. Their child, however, may be partial to the preferences of one parent over the other but does not completely reflect the style of either parent. In addition, siblings may learn differently from each other. Some may perform well in traditional settings, while others are more apt to do well in alternative learning environments.

Parents are the experts when it comes to their own children and probably will not be surprised to hear what their learner's preferences are. In addition, the assessment feedback can be a key factor in deterring those "sibling versus sibling" comparisons and "when I was in school" conversations that inevitably arise during some parent-teacher conferences.

These assessment tools can help to guide and keep a parent-teacher conversation as individualized as you hope your classroom may be. In addition, the guidance from the teacher and the help sheets provided by the Dunn and Dunn assessment are powerful tools for any parent to use in the home learning environment.

A word from the researcher

Rita Dunn on the impact of learning styles

In a 2007 interview at Ball State University, Dr. Rita Dunn commented on the impact of learning styles on her curriculum development, No Child Left Behind (NCLB), and on teacher preparation programs of the future. Dunn commented on how she used learning styles when she taught her own courses:

"...When I am teaching, I've got multisensory materials. I start globally. I tell them what my style is. I am collegial versus authoritative with different students. I never ask just for term papers, I mean, that's ridiculous. I make students develop materials. Portfolios—well that's one way. I have them make training materials for different learning styles for anything that they have to learn. So then, they can teach someone else. I let students who are so disposed write articles for publication. They have to write an article for publication persuading people with the research, with practical application, with documentation. Statistics—they're afraid of it. I get my students involved in a real project that I am doing, a real research paper. I teach them the statistics they need to know. That's not my educational specialty. They still have stringent requirements; they still have a final test. I had a doctoral student who went hysterical when she had to take statistics. She said, 'I'm not going to pass.' So I said, 'Remember your style. You're global.' I reminded her of what globals should do. And she passed. You just have to remind them what their strengths are."

When asked how learning styles related to the initiative of NCLB, she responded:

"No Child Left Behind [No Child Left Behind Act of 2001 Executive Summary, Pub. L. 107-110, retrieved August 17, 2004] is atrocious. I don't know where all my colleagues and educators are. [The] No Child Left Behind Act is a great icon or theory, just like multiple intelligence, a worthwhile construct, a worthwhile theory. It imposes periodic testing on every school. Show me a single study that shows that increased school testing increases achievement. It doesn't. In some cases, teachers spend more time on the subject, so maybe kids do better. It will make some teachers teach to the test. You know, I believe in testing. But you've got to change the instruction if you want increased achievement. [No Child Left Behind Act] has no strategies benefiting teachers. It doesn't tell them what to do. It makes teachers responsible for increased achievement. It doesn't tell the teachers how to do it—no prescription. George Bush could call Rita Dunn and say, 'We have limited funds. Tell me what to do.' And I would tell him exactly what to do. Learning styles. Make learning style testing part of every curriculum. It costs two dollars to test for learning styles. It comes with a prescription. Let teachers see how you do it. Let them see classrooms. There are so many positive things that can be done to improve the system."

And lastly, Rita Dunn had this to say when commenting on possible implications for teacher education relating to learning style research:

> "You know, we've got to train professors to make potential teachers alert to the fact that good ideas, interesting ideas, should be worked with on small pilot bases, not adopted wholesale. But what happens is that everyone wants to go to conferences. So they go to the major organizations who constantly promote new things because they are commercial [materials, companies] and make money from selling all these new things. And administrators who are not alert to the research adopt everything. There's an aura about 'We're doing this. This is new.' Why are you doing it? Show me the research on it. Why are you not just doing a pilot study with two classes to see if it really has impact? We don't train people like that."

These are not the words of a researcher, but a practitioner. Rita Dunn was a teacher in the trenches who tried to find effective ways for other teachers to achieve academic success. The issues within our educational system have not changed much since the late 1960s. There are still problems with literacy, retention, funding, accountability through state and national assessments, teacher preparation, parent involvement, etc. However, since that time, teachers with a desire for efficacy are still looking for solid solutions and can find them in this highly valuable model.

 *Conclusion*

Mr. Samson is doing a performance assessment of Newton's Three Laws of Motion in his classroom today. His students will move through three different stations to experience different activities that involve the application of Newton's laws to three different real-world problems. For each activity, the student will write a description of the application of all three of Newton's Laws of Motion. Mr. Samson has set up this highly mobile activity with the following specifics: the temperature of the room is moderate to warm, the lighting is more natural/dim, and there is music playing softly in the background. He has addressed responsibility by handing each student a checklist of tasks to be performed in sequence, and provided motivation by rewarding students who complete these assessments at a level of 80 percent or higher with playing online review games (such as *Jeopardy!*®, *Who Wants to Be a Millionaire?*, or matching terms at http://www.quia.com), or using sets of magnetic balls and beams, Lego® building bricks, Tinkertoys®, or Lincoln Logs™ to build structures using their new skills. If students score below an 80 percent on their assessments, they must participate in remediation activities to review the information. Mr. Samson has informed the students that they must participate in the performance assessments individually, but they may do the online review games, hands-on building activities, or remediation activities with partners. Students may have water and a snack, which must be kept at their desks, so they do not make a mess as they move from one station to the next. They may go to each station at their own pace to perform the task and then write their descriptions wherever they are most comfortable in the classroom (at their desk, in a beanbag chair at the reading station, on the floor, at a lab table, typing on a computer, etc.).

Think about it!

- In what ways has Mr. Samson appealed to both right- and left-brain learners?

- What environmental stimuli did Mr. Samson use? How do you suppose Mr. Samson decided which stimuli would be best for his class?

- Having a self-paced performance assessment appeals to which specific preferences?

- What aspects of emotional stimuli have been provided?

Chapter 3

Howard Gardner

Description

The Theory of Multiple Intelligences was developed in 1983 by Dr. Howard Gardner. Dr. Gardner is a professor of education at Harvard University. He was concerned about the conventional assessment of intelligence. He thought it focused too highly on mathematical-logical and language skills. His theory suggests that the traditional ideas of intelligence based on I.Q. testing are not encompassing enough to fully describe one's intelligence. He wanted to broaden the definition of intelligence. So instead, Dr. Gardner proposed eight different intelligences to fully describe one's intellect. In Gardner's Theory of Multiple Intelligences, he more accurately captures the diverse nature of human capability to learn in different areas.

According to Gardner, intelligence involves the ability to create a useful product, offer an appreciated service, possess a set of problem-solving skills, and find solutions to problems by gathering new knowledge. Gardner also believes that human beings possess all of the eight intelligences he has identified in varying amounts; these intelligences are located in different parts of the brain. These intelligences can either work alone or together with others. He also believes that education can be improved by addressing the multiple intelligences of students.

The eight intelligences identified by Howard Gardner are as follows:

Verbal-Linguistic (words)

Logical-Mathematical (numbers)

Visual-Spatial (pictures)

Bodily-Kinesthetic (body)

Rhythmic-Musical (music)

Interpersonal (people)

Intrapersonal (self)

Naturalist (nature)

History

Howard Gardner entered Harvard in 1961 with plans to major in history. But under the influence of Erik Erikson, he changed his major. Gardner became interested in social relations (a combination of psychology, sociology, and anthropology). He was particularly interested in clinical psychology. This branch of psychology deals with the diagnosis and treatment of psychological and behavioral problems. Gardner later changed his field of interest after meeting cognitive (study of mental states) psychologist Jerome Bruner and studying the writings of Jean Piaget.

After finishing his Ph.D. at Harvard in 1971 with a dissertation on style sensitivity in children, Gardner continued to work at Harvard with Nelson Goodman. They worked with a research team on Project Zero. Project Zero was founded at the Harvard Graduate School of Education in 1967 by Nelson Goodman. The focus of this project was to study and improve education in and through the arts.

In 1983, Gardner proposed his Theory of Multiple Intelligences. This theory was introduced to more correctly define intelligence and to address whether the techniques and measures that claim to determine intelligence are truly scientific. Howard Gardner viewed intelligence as the capacity to solve problems. He reviewed the research on intelligence using this list of eight different criteria (Gardner 1993, 62–69):

- potential isolation by brain damage
- the existence of idiot savants or other exceptional individuals
- an identifiable core of operations or set of operations
- a distinctive developmental history
- an evolutionary history and evolutionary plausibility
- support from experimental psychological tasks
- support from psychometric findings
- susceptibility to encoding in a symbol system

In 1999, Gardner initially developed a list of seven different intelligences: Verbal-Linguistic, Logical-Mathematical, Rhythmic-Musical, Bodily-Kinesthetic, Visual-Spatial, Interpersonal, and Intrapersonal. An eighth intelligence—Naturalist—was added later. Historically, the Verbal-Linguistic and Logical-Mathematical intelligences had been valued in school settings. Rhythmic-Musical, Bodily-Kinesthetic, and Visual-Spatial are often associated with the arts. Intrapersonal and Interpersonal intelligences are what Gardner called *personal intelligences*.

Gardner's intelligence theory has been highly scrutinized by the educational theory and psychology communities. They argue that Gardner's theory is based on his own intuition rather than data. Other arguments claim that these intelligences are substitute names for personality types. Despite these arguments against Gardner's intelligences, the theory has been widely accepted and welcomed by educators for the past 20 years. Many schools and individual teachers have incorporated some aspects of Gardner's intelligence research into their educational practices. Many schools and educators have structured curriculum according to Gardner's intelligences because they provide a framework for organizing curricula to better meet the needs of a wide range of learners.

Gardner supports that differences in the strengths of intelligences challenge typical educational systems that assume everyone learns the same way, at the same pace, using the same materials and methodologies. He adds that the wide variety of learners in today's classrooms could be better served if information and learning could be presented and assessed through a variety of different ways.

Application of this model for everyday classroom use and lesson planning

Howard Gardner's Theory of Multiple Intelligences makes people think about "IQ," about being "smart." His theory is changing the way some teachers teach. The focus is not how smart a student is, but *how* they are smart. Teachers are using knowledge of Multiple Intelligences to create learning activities better suited to the ways these individual students learn versus the one-size-fits-all style of traditional education.

When Gardner's book *Frames of Mind: The Theory of Multiple Intelligences* (1983) first came out, it seemed to answer many questions for experienced teachers. One burning question for experienced teachers was "Why do I have bright students who fail to perform well on exams?" Gardner's claim that there are several different kinds of intelligence gave both experienced teachers and novice teachers a way to begin to understand those "bright" students who performed poorly on tests. Teachers began to observe what those students could do well, instead of what they could not do.

Gardner wrote other books such as *The Unschooled Mind: How Children Think and How Schools Should Teach* (1991) and *Multiple Intelligences: The Theory in Practice* (1993) to help teachers understand how multiple intelligences could help them teach and evaluate students in new and improved ways.

When asked how educators should implement the Theory of Multiple Intelligences, Gardner says, "It's very important that a teacher take individual differences among kids very seriously…. The bottom line is a deep interest in children and how their minds are different from one another, and in helping them use their minds well" (1993). The first step to incorporate Gardner's research is to survey your students to find out their individual intelligences. A sample Multiple Intelligence Inventory can be found at http://www.ldrc.ca/projects/miinventory/miinventory.php. This survey can help educators identify the learning styles of their students.

Once teachers have identified the students' intelligences, they can incorporate this knowledge into lesson design, interdisciplinary units, student projects, individualized assessments, and apprenticeships. Some schools focus on lesson design. This might involve team teaching, using all or several of the intelligences in the lessons. Interdisciplinary units allow certain students to excel in a subject of their strength and foster deeper understanding through transfer between subjects. Through student projects, students can learn to initiate and manage complex tasks with a focus on teamwork. These are important real-world, workplace skills to possess. Individualized assessments allow students to show what they have learned. Sometimes the assessment allows each student to determine the way he or she will be assessed, while meeting the teacher's criteria for quality. Apprenticeships can allow students to gradually gain mastery of a trade or skill through real-life experience over time. Gardner feels that apprenticeships should take up about one-third of a student's schooling experience.

By understanding Gardner's Theory of Multiple Intelligences, teachers, school administrators, support personnel, and parents can better understand the variety of learners they deal with on a daily basis. With this knowledge, they can allow students to safely explore and learn in many different ways, and they can help students direct their own learning, since the instruction and learning activities are tailored to how the individual student learns best. Adults can help students understand and appreciate their strengths and identify real-world activities that will stimulate enhanced learning experiences.

The tables on the following pages describe the characteristics of each intelligence type, including what each type of learner does best, suggested areas of instructional focus, preferred learning strategies, and preferred learning products. It should be noted that Gardner does not specify a preferred learning environment for each intelligence type. Awareness of each individual intelligence style's characteristics will assist educators in developing a variety of learning activities suited to each style.

Verbal-Linguistic

Characteristics	Preferred learning strategies
• excellent language skills • outstanding communicators • speak and write exceptionally well	• learn best by reading and taking notes • learn best by listening to lectures and discussions • benefit from computer use
What do these learners do best? • read • write • talk • memorize information • think in words	**Preferred learning products** • demonstrations • interviews • oral reports • pamphlets • journals
Instructional focus • reading • hearing information • discussing topics • writing • debating	

Student profile: Nick is a typical Verbal-Linguistic learner. He loves a great debate and is the first one to ask the difficult question for all to ponder. Nick has no qualms about speaking in front of the group—in fact, he revels in these types of opportunities. He wants to be a lawyer.

Logical-Mathematical

Characteristics	Preferred learning strategies
• able to recognize relationships and patterns between concepts and objects • logical thinkers • problem solvers	• learn best through experimentation and problem solving
What do these learners do best?	**Preferred learning products**
• solve problems • experiment • ask questions • research information • reason	• models • mobiles • computer programs • charts • labeled diagrams • large-scale drawings
Instructional focus • classifying information • categorizing information • working with the abstract • working with patterns and relationships	

Student profile: Zachary is the textbook Logical-Mathematical learner. He is the first to solve difficult problems. Zach loves challenging assignments and can produce excellent charts and diagrams to illustrate data he has collected from extensive research activities. He wants to go into engineering or drafting as a career.

Visual-Spatial

Characteristics	Preferred learning strategies
• strong visual and spatial ideas • think in images • very aware of surroundings	• learn best by visualizing and mentally manipulating information
What do these learners do best?	**Preferred learning products**
• design • draw • dream • create • construct	• bulletin boards • graphs • illustrated stories • murals • displays • charts • slide shows
Instructional focus • visualizing information • drawing • working with pictures	
Student profile: Jolie is a prime example of a Visual-Spatial learner. She loves to create visual displays of her learning activities. Her productions are clear and often aid others in better understanding difficult concepts. Jolie wants to be an architect.	

Bodily-Kinesthetic

Characteristics	Preferred learning strategies
• able to use one's body skillfully • easily able to manipulate objects • athletic • keen sense of body awareness	• learn best by doing something physically over reading or writing about it • learn better by getting up and moving around
What do these learners do best?	**Preferred learning products**
• physical activity • dancing • arts and crafts • manipulating tools • communicate well through body language	• plays • charades • demonstrations • painting • experiments • pantomimes • role playing
Instructional focus	
• processing information through body sensations • tactile manipulatives • hands-on experiments/activities	

Student profile: Kelli is a Bodily-Kinesthetic learner. She loves hands-on activities and is a very good athlete. Kelli excels in demonstrating learning concepts and enjoys experimenting, too. She plans to be a college athlete and go into education. Kelli wants to focus on hands-on learning throughout her teaching career.

Rhythmic-Musical

Characteristics	Preferred learning strategies
• musical • appreciate a variety of musical forms • perceptive to rhythm, melody, and pitch	• may learn best through listening to lectures • enjoy using songs or rhythms to learn or memorize information • may study better with music in the background
What do these learners do best? • sing • remember melodies • pick up sound and rhythms	**Preferred learning products** • instrumentals • audiovisuals • raps • songs • poems • videos
Instructional focus • listening to music • singing • rhythmic mnemonic devices	

Student profile: Ian is the band club president. He plays the guitar and piano and can sing extremely well. Ian loves the opportunity to create songs to describe learning concepts and isn't afraid to perform his creative work in front of the class. Ian wants to be a famous pop artist.

Interpersonal

Characteristics	Preferred learning strategies
• understand others quite well • great communication skills • empathetic	• learn best by working with others • enjoy debates and discussions • benefit from videoconferencing, email, etc.
What do these learners do best? • interact with people • lead activities • communicate with others • work in groups	**Preferred learning products** • debates • editorial essay • interviews • journals • plays • TV programs
Instructional focus • cooperative groups • interviews with other people • sharing information	

Student profile: Kathy is very empathetic. She understands the actions of others very well and works well with all students. Kathy is very popular and is involved in many school clubs and activities. Her favorite learning activities involve group work. She is the first to volunteer to help out. Kathy plans to be a nurse.

Intrapersonal

Characteristics	Preferred learning strategies
• in touch with own self • intuitive • independent	• learn best when allowed to concentrate on the subject individually
What do these learners do best?	**Preferred learning products**
• set goals • know own strengths and weaknesses • understand self • self-reflect	• diaries • journals • timelines • charts • learning centers
Instructional focus	
• working alone • self-paced individual projects • reflection of one's work • intrinsic motivation	

Student profile: Matt is very self-motivated. He is intrigued with scientific research. He likes to work alone to solve problems. Matt keeps detailed records and is the first to volunteer to be the lead participant in group lab work. Matt plans to go into medical research. He wants to find the cure for cancer.

Naturalist

Characteristics	Preferred learning strategies
• nature lover • environmentally aware	• learn best when the activity involves collecting and analyzing • learn best in outdoor settings • enjoy kinesthetic activities
What do these learners do best? • identify and classify environmental components	**Preferred learning products** • field studies • artifact collections • leaf collections • field trips • dioramas
Instructional focus • classify • analyze	

Student profile: Marc loves any outdoor activity. He has many collections consisting of leaves, rocks, fossils, plants, etc. Marc has a special interest in medicinal plants. Someday, he plans to live and work in the Amazon rain forest.

What can a teacher do with this information?

Traditionally, education systems have stressed the development and use of verbal and mathematical intelligences. The Theory of Multiple Intelligences suggests that educators should identify and tailor instruction to a wider range of talents and skills involving the eight different intelligences Gardner has identified.

Teaching to all learning styles may seem daunting, but the key is to include as many different learning style activities as possible in any given lesson. When presenting information to students, teachers should try to incorporate delivery methods that target as many of the intelligences as possible. For example, when teaching a lesson on global warming, instructors may show data tables and graphs of various regions of the Earth, show video clips of areas affected by global warming, monitor a debate on the topic, encourage students to develop a documentary, provide art materials for students to create comic strips or posters depicting global warming effects, and facilitate research projects on the issue. A variety of learning activities not only engages the students, but also allows the teacher flexibility in facilitating the learning objectives.

Providing choices of activities based on intelligences allows teachers to incorporate a wide variety of activities on a daily basis. Using visuals, printed words, audio, motion, and multimedia assists in addressing to the different intelligences. By activating a wide variety of intelligences, teachers help students gain a deeper understanding of the subject material.

The multiple intelligences product grid (Taylor 2002) shown on pages 79–80 is an overview of possible learning activities that parallel Gardner's intelligences. The grid provides instructors with a large variety of activity choices that align with different learning styles.

Multiple intelligences product grid

Verbal-Linguistic	Logical-Mathematical	Visual-Spatial	Bodily-Kinesthetic
advertisement	advertisement	animated movie	calligraphy
annotated bibliography	annotated bibliography	art gallery	charades
bulletin board	chart	bulletin board	collage
code	code	bumper sticker	costumes
comic strip	collage	cartoon	dance
debate	collection	chart	demonstration
demonstration	computer program	clay sculpture	diorama
diary	crossword puzzle	collage	etching
editorial essay	database	costumes	experiment
fairy tale	debate	demonstration	film
family tree	demonstration	diorama	flip-book
fiction story	detailed illustration	display	food
interview	edibles	etching	hidden picture
jingle	experiment	film	mosaic
joke book	fact file	filmstrip	mural
journal	family tree	flipbook	musical
lesson	game	game	musical instrument
letter	graph	graph	needlework
letter to the editor	hidden picture	hidden picture	painting
newspaper story	labeled diagram	illustrated story	pantomime
nonfiction	large-scale drawing	maze	papier mâché
oral defense	lesson	mobile	plaster of Paris
oral report	map with legend	model	model
pamphlet	maze	mosaic	play
petition	mobile	mural	poem
play	model	painting	press conference
poem	petition	papier mâché	puppet
press conference	play	photo essay	puppet show
radio program	prototype	pictures	radio program
riddle	puzzle	picture story for	role play
science fiction story	recipe	children	transparencies
skit	riddle	play	television program
slogan	survey	political cartoon	
soliloquy	timeline	pop-up book	
story telling	transparencies	prototype	
television program	Venn diagram	rebus story	
write a new law	working hypothesis	slide show	
	write a new law	story cube	
		transparencies	
		travel brochure	
		television program	
		web home page	

Multiple intelligences product grid *(cont.)*

Rhythmic-Musical	Interpersonal	Intrapersonal	Naturalist
audio-video tape	advertisement	bulletin board	artifact collecting
choral reading	animated movie	chart	diorama
fairy tale	bulletin board	collection	field study
film	chart	comic strip	field trip
instrumental	choral reading	diary	fossil collecting
jukebox	comic strip	editorial essay	insect collecting
musical	debate	fairy tale	leaf collecting
poem	demonstration	family tree	original song
rap song	editorial essay	journal	photo essay
riddle	fairy tale	learning center	rock collection
role playing	film game	poem	scientific drawing
song	interview	riddle maze collage	spelunking trip
sound	journal	timeline	timeline
	lesson		
	maze		
	museum exhibit		
	pamphlet		
	petition		
	play		
	press conference		
	role playing		
	television program		
	write a new law		

Sample activities for each learning style

The setting:

In an elementary classroom, the students are expected to perform the computational procedures: add and subtract fractions (like and unlike denominators) greater than or equal to zero (including mixed numbers) without regrouping and without expressing answers in simplest form. Ms. Myers has created numerous learning activities aligned with Gardner's Multiple Intelligences for her students to help them learn how to add and subtract fractions.

Activity #1: Story/Worksheet

Learning preference: Verbal-Linguistic

Description: Teacher reads aloud *The Hershey's® Milk Chocolate Bar Fractions Book* by Jerry Pallotta (1999). All children should have a Hershey's® 12-piece chocolate bar to break into pieces when told to do so as the book is read. After the story, complete a short fraction worksheet.

Accommodations for special needs populations:

English language learners: Pair these students with other language proficient students to complete the fraction worksheet.

Above-level learners: Encourage these students to read part of the story out loud to the rest of the class.

Below-level learners: Provide these learners with visuals. Allow the work to match the strength of the learner.

Varying instructional methods according to grade level:

Elementary level: This activity is well suited for upper-elementary-level students. Younger elementary students could do similar math-related activities, such as counting books with accompanying activities.

Intermediate level: This student may benefit from similar hands-on activities involving food and adding or subtracting fractions. The story should be age appropriate and the fraction manipulations should be more challenging for this level.

Secondary level: These upper-level students could create their own math-related stories pertaining to surface area, graphing equations, or engineering concepts to read to the class.

Activity #2: Cookie Recipe

Learning preference: Logical/Mathematical

Description: Add or subtract the fractions on the cookie recipe to fit the needs of your class. Use your answers to make the no-bake cookies.

Accommodations for special needs populations:

English language learners: Since these learners respond well to kinesthetic activities, allow them to provide verbal explanations of the recipe manipulations rather than write them down.

Above-level learners: Challenge these students to alter a recipe to accommodate a larger group of people.

Below-level learners: Provide these students with a partial recipe to complete.

Varying instructional methods according to grade level:

Elementary level: This student will need much assistance with altering the cookie recipe. Provide guidelines for them to follow and go through the recipe process with the entire group.

Intermediate level: Provide these students with the recipe and also tell them how many students the recipe should serve. For instance, if the recipe calls for two dozen and the class will actually need four dozen, then students need to double the recipe.

Secondary level: For this student, make the activity a party-planning event, with students bringing in their favorite recipes and altering each recipe according to class needs.

Activity #3: Flashcards

Learning preference: Visual/Spatial

Description: Use flash cards to practice finding the least common denominator. Two fractions are listed on the front of each card and their LCD is on the back.

Accommodations for special needs populations:

English language learners: Using visual flashcards and repeated practice with visual aids provides an effective learning tool for this type of learner.

Above-level learners: Challenge these students to create their own flashcards or develop flashcard sets for the entire class to use.

Below-level learners: These students will also benefit from the use of flashcards as this allows adequate time for practice. Pair them with students of similar ability level so they will not feel intimidated or pressured to rush through the process.

Varying instructional methods according to grade level:

Elementary level: Make sure the math flashcards contain age-appropriate content. Teachers may work at learning centers with small groups of students to go through the flashcards containing the math facts.

Intermediate level: Pair students carefully as they practice the flashcards. Allowing students to choose their own partners often leads to more socializing than content mastery, so be cautious of allowing students to choose their own partners or groups. Students at the middle school level also seem more susceptible to feeling the pressures of "fitting in" and may need incentives to take the assignment seriously.

Secondary level: Although older, these students still benefit from the practice of using flashcards.

Activity #4: Poker Chip Activity

Learning preference: Bodily/Kinesthetic

Description: Using poker chips and large hand-drawn or plastic circles, place chips in circles to illustrate the mixed number fractions in problems from an accompanying worksheet.

Accommodations for special needs populations:

English language learners: The kinesthetic learning activities allow students to provide verbal explanations while they arrange the poker chips in the circles to illustrate the mixed number fractions.

Above-level learners: Provide these learners with challenging problems to illustrate throughout the activity.

Below-level learners: These students profit from working in small groups to carry out additional practice with skills that are difficult for them.

Varying instructional methods according to grade level:

Elementary level: Depending on the elementary grade level, ask students to use colors to shade in particular pictures to represent mixed numbers.

Shade in $\frac{3}{3}$ of this shape.   Shade in $\frac{1}{3}$ of this shape.

Intermediate level: This student will enjoy an additional hands-on activity of drawing pictures to illustrate mixed numbers. These pictures may be representative of their favorite things to add a more personal touch to the activity.

Secondary level: Challenge these students to collect class data over specific topics and change the fractions of the data to mixed numbers or vice versa.

··

Activity #5: Fraction Song

Learning preference: Rhythmic/Musical

Description: Create a song about adding and subtracting fractions. Play your own music or use audio samples provided by your teacher.

Accommodations for special needs populations:

English language learners: These students may benefit from adding personal content to their fraction song. In addition, pair ELL students with language proficient students.

Above-level learners: Challenge these students by incorporating real-life data into their fraction song and encouraging them to perform their song to the entire class.

Below-level learners: Allow these students the opportunity to work in small groups to create a song through a collaborative effort.

Varying instructional methods according to grade level:

Elementary level: Adding educational content to familiar tunes such as "Row, Row, Row Your Boat" and "Mary Had a Little Lamb" is appropriate for elementary students.

Intermediate level: This student enjoys adding or changing lyrics to raps and popular music.

Secondary level: Provide these students the choice of creating a rap, song, or poem that incorporates math concepts, and then ask them to perform it for the class.

Activity #6: Fraction Card Game

Learning preference: Interpersonal

Description: Play a fraction card game. Deal cards out to players. Students make pairs of cards containing fractions that add up to one.

Accommodations for special needs populations:

English language learners: Allow these learners to use manipulatives to help illustrate learning concepts. As students play the game, promote open dialogue, which is also helpful for these learners.

Above-level learners: Encourage these students to use their creative talents to draw representative pictures of the fractions.

Below-level learners: These students may require strong teacher guidance. Allow the work to match the strength of the learner(s).

Varying instructional methods according to grade level:

Elementary level: According to the elementary grade level, vary the difficulty of the fractions that are used to add up to one.

Intermediate level: A more difficult game of Fraction Rummy may be more suitable for this level. Deal cards one at a time in a clockwise manner so each player gets seven cards. Place the deck in the center and turn up a single card as a waste pile. Play continues around the group as in traditional rummy (take a card and make a discard). The object is to get a group of either three or four cards that are equivalent or a group of three or four cards with the same denominator.

Secondary level: Encourage these students to create a card game for middle or elementary school students that covers similar math concepts.

Activity #7: Interactive Computer Lab

Learning preference: Intrapersonal

Description: Complete a computer lab and fill in the recording sheet that goes with the lab.

Accommodations for special needs populations:

English language learners: The visual aids presented on interactive computer games is a benefit for these learners.

Above-level learners: Impose a time limit upon these students for an additional challenge.

Below-level learners: Afford these students the option of going through the cards multiple times for mastery.

Varying instructional methods according to grade level:

Elementary level: The quiz noted above is for the elementary level.

Intermediate level: A similar quiz appropriate for middle level learners may be found at: http://www.glencoe.com/sec/math/studytools/cgi-bin/msgQuiz.php4?isbn=0-07-874042-8&chapter=4&lesson=0&headerFile=7

Secondary level: Numerous interactive quizzes are available online. Find the quiz that correlates to the math topic and assign the online quiz to students. At this grade level, the student craves immediate feedback, which these activities provide.

Activity #8: Leaf Collection

Learning preference: Naturalist

Description: Collect a group of leaves from the schoolyard. Sort the leaves and add up the different kinds, then ask students to determine the fraction of each variety out of the total number of leaves collected. If it is not the appropriate season for leaf collection, provide paper or picture samples of various leaves for students to identify and group.

Accommodations for special needs populations:

English language learners: The hands-on kinesthetic nature of this activity allows ELL students to show what they know without having to use extensive language skills.

Above-level learners: Ask these students to collect and identify at least 10 different kinds of leaves for their collections.

Below-level learners: Assign fewer leaves to collect, identify, and arrange into fractions.

Varying instructional methods according to grade level:

Elementary level: Collect an even number of leaves for this activity and work as a class to add up the different varieties and determine simple fractions accordingly.

Intermediate level: At this level, students could work individually or in small groups to collect a variety of leaves, compile the data, and present this data to the class.

Secondary level: Encourage these students to conduct biodiversity studies on particular plots of land in the schoolyard and collect, analyze, and report data.

Teachers and parents working together to accommodate these learning styles

Teachers should encourage parents to observe their children at home during homework time to decide what type of learner their child is. Teachers should also encourage parents to ask them, counselors, and administrators for learning style assessment feedback on their child. Children and parents may work together as children carry out online intelligence assessments so parents will have background knowledge of their child's learning style(s). Once parents know what kind of learner their child is, they can develop and foster activities at home that make the most of their child's strengths and abilities. The next page shows suggestions for providing home support that teachers can make to parents according to the learning style of their child.

How to offer home support

Verbal-Linguistic learners	Logical-Mathematical learners
• Read with your child and provide books for them to read and use for reference materials. • Listen closely to your child's questions, concerns, and experiences. • Encourage verbal/linguistic learners to summarize stories they have read or written. • Take your child to the library and bookstores often, and play games such as Scrabble® and Boggle® to enhance their skills.	• Play number, pattern, and problem-solving games with your child. • Foster their strong reasoning skills and be attentive to their questions posed in a logical manner. • Let the child experiment and invite him or her to help out with the cooking. • Assign tasks such as setting the table, sorting clothes, or organizing drawers or cabinets.
Visual-Spatial learners	**Rhythmic-Musical learners**
• Students need a wide variety of resources to create arts and crafts. • Allow opportunities for children to solve puzzles, visit art museums, or take family photos. • They enjoy playing card games. • Be respectful of the fact that these children may be daydreamers.	• Be prepared to provide access to a variety of musical instruments for the child to play. • Music lessons are also very beneficial for these learners. • Attend concerts and musicals when possible. • Encourage these children to sing and clap to the rhythm of music and have sing-alongs with them to foster their learning style.
Bodily-Kinesthetic learners	**Interpersonal learners**
• Involve students in dancing, acting, or sports activities. • Family walks, hikes, jogs, or sports activities enhance their thinking and learning skills. • Try to provide a variety of manipulatives for children to carry out experiments at home. • Play games with them like Twister® and charades.	• Play family games and foster family discussions and problem solving. • Encourage these children to help out their peers and work cooperatively with others. • Respect the fact that these children are social beings, so provide opporunities for such interactions.

How to offer home support (cont.)

Intrapersonal learners	Naturalist learners
• Intrapersonal learners like to work independently, so offer them opportunities to work or play alone. • Encourage these children to keep a journal, diary, or family log. • Respect the fact that these learners "march to the beat of a different drummer."	• Provide outdoor experiences whenever possible. • Take these children for walks in the park, nature hikes, or any other outdoor setting activity. • Support the child's need to create collections of rocks, leaves, outdoor treasures, etc. • Be respectful of the fact that it may be difficult for the child to stay inside for long periods of time.

By talking with parents about personal learning styles, teachers will strengthen the lines of communication with them. Most parents respect efforts by a teacher to go the extra mile in determining how their child learns best. Sharing the above information is a win-win situation for all involved—the student, the teacher, and the parent.

 *Conclusion*

Once again, it's a busy day in Mr. Kimmel's biology class. Students are studying cells. As a firm believer in incorporating Gardner's Theory of Multiple Intelligences, Mr. Kimmel consistently incorporates a variety of learning activities for his biology students. He likes to use a variety of stations to engage learners in a myriad of activities aligned with the eight different learning styles identified by Howard Gardner. He directs students to first complete the learning activities in the stations aligned with their learning style strengths and then choose from any of the other stations as they carry out learning activities.

Station	Activity
Station #1:	Students choose to create a cell model or a mobile. The station is equipped with a variety of art materials.
Station #2:	Students choose to create a pamphlet or a journal entry that pertains to the various organelles of the cell and their functions.
Station #3:	Students can create a rap or a song with lyrics associated with the various cell organelles and their functions.
Station #4:	The task at this station is to collect plant samples and study thin layers of plant matter under the microscope. Students will then compare plant and animal cell structures.
Station #5:	Students choose to conduct an interview involving cells with a professional in the field or to write an editorial discussing how to keep one's cells healthy.
Station #6:	Students create a bulletin board illustrating comparisons of animal and plant cells.
Station #7:	Students will carry out a cheek cell lab at this station. They will collect, stain, and examine cheek cells under the microscope.
Station #8:	Students choose to create a timeline of major cell discoveries or carry out an interactive quiz involving the cell organelles and their functions.

Think about it!

- Which station is tailored for Intrapersonal learners? Verbal-Linguistic? Visual-Spatial? Naturalist? Rhythmic-Musical? Interpersonal? Bodily-Kinesthetic? Logical-Mathematical?

- Would you prefer all students to rotate through all stations or match them with the station that fits their learning style strengths? How about providing students with an overall choice of which activities they prefer to carry out?

- How has the teacher both differentiated and tailored instruction according to Gardner's learning styles?

- How would you communicate the purpose of these stations to your administrator, colleagues, and parents?

Chapter 4

Neil Fleming and the VARK Learning Styles Model

Description

The phrase "I'm different, not dumb" reflects the basic belief present throughout Neil Fleming's written contributions to the learning style community. Fleming is the creator of the VARK model. VARK stands for *visual*, *aural*, *read-write*, and *kinesthetic*. The VARK Learning Style model represents one preference: the mode of perceiving information in a learning context. This system addresses how individuals take in and put out information. By utilizing a simple 16-question assessment tool, users obtain a profile of their preferences and have access to information about how to enhance their own learning using the strengths indicated by the questionnaire. The questionnaire and applicable resources are found free of charge and online at http://www.vark-learn.com. The VARK has gained most of its fame from its short questionnaire with simple, easy-to-understand results.

In just under 10 minutes, an individual of any age can find out if he or she is visual, aural, read-write, kinesthetic, or a combination of these styles, which is known as being *multimodal*. The assessment tool does not include "right" or "wrong" answers, is short enough not to bore or disengage the person taking it, and provides ready-to-use advice for the learner to implement immediately. A unique aspect of the questionnaire is that the questions are based on situations in which the learner has choices or decisions as to what the next step in communication might be for them personally.

Fleming argues that most teachers conduct their classrooms using the mode that fits the teacher best, but they need to switch modes during instruction to appeal to all modes present in their classrooms. In addition, students should learn the most difficult concepts in their preferred mode, practice concepts that come easily in other modes, and be trusted to explore activities that are multi-modal.

In summary, the three basic principles of VARK include:

- Each person can learn but may do so differently despite the level of his or her ability.
- When a student's learning preference is accommodated, his or her level of motivation increases.
- It is best to present new material within the context of a learner's preferred mode of perception.

It is strongly suggested that a teacher take the questionnaire first to learn his or her own preference(s). Although a teacher may discover his or her own personal learning preference, research shows that he or she may not necessarily always teach that way. The educational system is so deeply rooted in the Read-Write preference that teachers will rely on it to transmit information to their students.

However, in today's classroom where teachers can no longer be the givers of all knowledge because resources for information are at their student's fingertips, an approach that is more multimodal may be more successful. A read-write preference is not necessarily bad if the teacher and students both have preferences for that mode of learning. The most positive results from VARK have come from situations in which the teacher has been matched with students that share the same mode preferences. A summary of each VARK mode is presented in the tables on the following pages, including the characteristics of each type of learner, his or her preferred learning strategies, what these learners do best, the preferred learning products, and the recommended learning focus. The VARK profile does not include a preference for learning environment in these descriptions.

Visual

Characteristics	Preferred learning strategies
• learn through visual depictions of graphs, flow charts, symbolic arrows, circles, hierarchies, and other devices to represent what can also be presented aurally	• underlining, using different color highlighters • reconstruct lecture using pictures and diagrams
What do these learners do best?	**Preferred learning products**
• see the big picture • apply visual representations to thought processes	• charts • posters • graphics • multimedia
Instructional focus • different colors • highlighters • symbols • flowcharts • graphs • pictures, videos, posters • texts with diagrams and pictures • lecturers who use gestures and lots of body language to emphasize a point	

Student profile: Jane is a visual learner. She responds very well to classroom demonstrations and graphics on presentations. To complete a project, she may ask to see past examples of a finished product beforehand to give her an idea of the task at hand. Once she has seen an example, engaging Jane and asking her to carry out tasks to apply her learning will be easy.

Aural

Characteristics	Preferred learning products
• prefer to learn through information that is "heard"	• MP3 players • audio versions of texts (audio books and CDs)

What do these learners do best?	Preferred learning strategies
• lectures, tutorials, and talking to other students • listen as information is explained to them	• discussions and tutorials • explain topics to others • remember story-based examples • summarize notes onto audio recordings and listen to them • read notes aloud • transpose lecture/study notes into discussions or tutorials

Instructional focus	
• attend lectures • narrated online tutorials • discuss topics with other students and/or lecturers • explain new ideas to other people • use a tape recorder to remember the interesting examples, stories, and jokes • leave spaces in your lecture notes for later recall and filling in information	

Student Profile: Louis never takes notes in class but is responsive in a classroom discussion. He makes statements such as "Can I just tell you what I've learned instead of writing it down?" This student is not lazy or lacking writing skills; his preference is for learning and demonstrating knowledge through conversation. Both oral and written communication skills should be options for this student to demonstrate his knowledge level.

Read-Write

Characteristics	Preferred learning products
• prefer to learn through information displayed as words • many academics have a strong preference for this mode	• notebooks with tabs • journals • note cards • word walls • posters with directions or key points

What do these learners do best?	Preferred learning strategies
• follow written directions • write essays and step-by-step directions • organize notes • make lists	• rewrite notes • make notes • read notes over again • describe pictures and diagrams in your own words • use lists, headings, etc. • arrange items into hierarchies with bullet points

Instructional focus
- lists
- definitions
- handouts
- textbooks
- lecture notes
- step-by-step procedures

Student profile: Maggie prefers to learn mainly by reading and writing. She usually wants to work individually instead of in pairs or a group. Maggie takes her time interpreting concepts, and until she prompts you for questions, she prefers to be left alone to analyze the information. Maggie will struggle when expectations for an assignment are more open-ended and not specific or are not written down in a format that can be easily followed. She may show frustration in those circumstances.

Kinesthetic

Characteristics	Preferred learning products
• learns through experience and practice (simulated or real) • student is connected to reality, either through experience, example, practice, or simulation	• specimens • manipulatives • live demonstrations • labs
What do these learners do best?	**Preferred learning strategies**
• need to do things to understand • manipulate objects • build or construct • hands-on projects • finding solutions to problems	• case studies and real-life applications to help with abstract concepts • talk about notes with another person • use pictures or photographs to illustrate an idea
Instructional focus	
• use all senses—sight, touch, taste, smell, hearing • experiments • field trips • real-life examples and applications • hands-on approaches • trial and error • collections of samples (e.g., rock types, plants, insects) • exhibits, samples, photographs	

Student profile: Jason is a kinesthetic learner who relishes hands-on projects that apply to real-life problem solving. Jason rarely turns in his papers on time and, in fact, usually misplaces them. However, he prefers open-ended projects, thinks "outside the box," and is very persistent in seeing that what he creates actually works.

History

Neil Fleming developed the VARK model in 1987. Fleming has been teaching for over 40 years. His duties have included teaching positions with Lincoln University in New Zealand, at times concurrently with secondary and teacher education responsibilities. In the spring and fall, he provides workshops in North America, Asia, and Europe. In addition, his work has involved him with the sports world where he has worked with elite coaches to utilize the VARK approach in coaching.

Although this model has not been established as long as others, VARK is continually researched and analyzed. It is a close relationship to Gardner's Theory of Multiple Intelligences which includes some of the VARK preferences named as intelligences. But Gardner used five other dimensions to expand on each of them. As stated on http://www.vark-learn.com, the official VARK website, "Sometimes the link between VARK and these theories appears to be quite strong, but VARK has its own focus, rationale, and strategies."

VARK is not a learning style on its own. The term "learning style" is technically what refers to all elements that might affect a person's ability to perceive and ingest information. Some "learning style" surveys focus on many components (as seen in the Dunn and Dunn model), including environmental aspects that can affect the learning process, while there are also personality-based surveys that use preferences for learning as a part of their diagnostic for entire personality types.

In contrast, VARK is limited to the mode of perception of information, mainly because Fleming had the most success when using that particular type of information to assist his learners. While appealing to other dimensions may have an effect, he saw that the most direct correlation for efficient learning is with the modal preferences.

Application of this model for everyday classroom use and lesson planning

Fleming understands well the paradigm shift that must occur for students to learn at the highest capacity. He emphasizes using an objective-based curriculum that is deeply rooted in problem solving and is multimodal in nature. His research discusses similar elements to those found in discussions of the 21st century classroom. For example, it isn't as important for students to memorize information as it is for them to know how to *find* the information.

At the same time, Fleming understands the barriers that teachers confront every day in modern education. Those barriers (heavy work load, increased student population, stringent content objectives with high-stakes assessments looming overhead, etc.) may not change, but the approach to them can. Teachers can break down these barriers and find more success by fostering skills such as learning by doing, independent learning, project work, and reflection when they are armed with a "learning identity" for themselves and their students. Allow your students to be a fluid and continuous part of conversations on how to learn, practice, and assess the objectives you must cover.

Fleming refers to Kugel in his *From Teaching to Learning* workshop (1993). Kugel explains that there are five stages in the life of a teacher. The first stage (we may be familiar with, but would rather forget) is "Will I survive?" This relates to the experience of the first year or two in a teaching career. A teacher is mainly focused on teaching at this point. Once a teacher has established survival, he or she moves more deeply into content during the third and fourth years. This stage is called, "I love this subject!" The focus is still on the teaching.

By approximately the fifth year, teachers reach the third stage, recognizing that "the learners seem to be different!" At this point, the teacher is not as focused on what *he or she* is doing (teaching), but is becoming more aware of what the *students* are doing (learning). This moves the open-minded and motivated teacher directly into the fourth stage, "Are they learning?" A teacher may start to explore research-based methods to assess whether his or her students are learning efficiently and how he or she can be a more effective teacher.

During this exploration, the teacher moves into the mode of classroom facilitator, which is the level of the master teacher— one who is in stage five, to which "students seem to be learning without me talking." The teacher realizes that it is more important for the students to *do* than for the teacher to *say* and has successfully moved from a "teacher-focused" to a "learner-focused" classroom.

A teacher in this final stage usually demonstrates the following characteristics:

- shows interest in how students learn
- encourages students to interact with each other
- uses questioning strategies that give credit to student contributions
- finds out what students know before starting to teach
- writes objectives from the student's point of view
- provides students with examples of work that is of the highest quality to demonstrate the requirements of the assignment
- makes grading criteria very clear
- gathers feedback from students regularly (see Appendix 6.5, page 171, for an example of our feedback survey)
- uses student-created questions

So, how does one get started in this model? First of all, visit http://www.vark-learn.com and take the online questionnaire. Once you have done so and know what to expect, you may then direct your students to do the same. Some tips for giving the VARK questionnaire and then discussing the results are offered on the next page.

1. The VARK questionnaire indicates preferences, not strengths. Be sure that is clear to students. Students may score low in the visual preference, and then claim they are visual people or that they enjoy reading. However, these same students may not like to draw or visit art galleries. Remember, VARK only shows the preferences for one mode in terms of the input and output of information.

2. The age of an individual makes a difference in the results. As one ages, one's experiences in work and life may diminish the boundaries between different modes, making one more adaptable to perceiving information in many different modes, thus becoming multi-modal.

3. Have a one-on-one conversation with each student to discuss his or her results. Some students may disagree with the preferred mode or modes shown in their results simply because they do not understand what qualifies them as a visual or aural learner. You can redirect the conversation by asking these students about the importance of color in their lives, and if they would prefer to gather information from a flowchart versus a page of writing, and so on.

4. Take students through the lists of strategies that are available to them after they complete the questionnaire. Refer to these lists often as students begin new content, need direction on study skills that would be most appropriate for them, and even review the test-taking strategies. In addition, discuss with and encourage students to apply these skills to other classes, as well.

5. Multi-modal students may need to try learning strategies that they have never tried before. These students will be much more successful if they develop a wide range of strategies based within their preferences.

What can a teacher do with this information?

First, the teacher needs to evaluate his or her own mode of learning. There are many helpful tips for teachers to use when exploring their own VARK mode(s) of learning. The following applies to the teacher and shows his or her preferences for disseminating information, as well as gathering information to assess his or her students' progress.

VARK mode of preference	This teacher prefers:	This teacher will use these strategies:
Visual	• visual aids to explain things • web pages that have strong graphics, hot boxes, etc. • diagrams, slides, charts, graphs, etc. • seeing complex ideas in a diagram or flowchart first • important words and ideas in a scattered pattern to increase interest • videos • exam questions with words like *illustrate, show, outline, label, link,* and *compare*	• concept maps • diagrams, models, flowcharts, etc. • computer animations • videos; slides; photographs to explicate, to clarify, or guide discussion
Aural	• explanations via tapes, conversations, phone calls, and/or discussions • opportunities for students to discuss among one another, work together, and contribute their own ideas. • clever use of speech to emphasize a point • student argument or debate • seminars, oral exams, group presentations, and dialogue • group work engrossed in planning and discussing ideas • exam questions with words like *explain, describe, discuss* and *state*	• audiotapes • class debates • student discussions • think-pair-share • small/large groups • brainstorming • guided lectures • group presentations

VARK mode of preference	This teacher prefers:	This teacher will use these strategies:
Read-Write	• text to explain things • handouts • reading articles before discussing them in class • argument and discussion in written text • important words placed on the board or overhead • words placed in a prioritized fashion • lists of points in a table format • essay exams • exam questions with words like *define, develop the case for, justify, analyze*	• quick writes • summaries • case studies • journals • student-created exams • formative quizzes • analytical lists • round table response • peer-to-peer review of notes
Kinesthetic	• real-life examples to explain things • offering a global view through guest lecturers, case studies, field trips and laboratories, exhibits, samples, newspaper stories, etc. • metaphors, examples, and analogies • props in class to highlight a point • role plays, demonstrations, practical tests, lab tests, and reports • texts that are filled with case studies, dialogues, narratives, biographies, and real-life situations • exam questions with words like *use examples, apply, demonstrate, construct, experience, dissect, develop, show*	• role playing • performances and skits • physical representations (e.g., parts of the body, government, etc.) • create physical models • evaluate a problem • plot information in a table, develop a graph, etc. • "thumbs up /thumbs down" or "stand up /sit down"

(NTL Forum 1998)

Next, teachers can apply their knowledge of the VARK modes to the classroom. According to T.A. Angelo's *A Teacher's Dozen* (1993), there are 14 research findings that can help teachers understand and improve their craft:

Students learn more when they...	Application to VARK
...are zealously engaged in their academic work.	If students are learning in their preferred mode, they are more apt to remain engaged.
...set and sustain high but realistic expectations and goals.	Reaching these expectations and goals will seem more accessible to the learner who is given the opportunity to utilize his or her strengths.
...provide, obtain, and make use of regular, timely, detailed feedback.	The more individualized (via learning mode) this feedback is, the more effective it will be for the learner.
...learn to direct their attention on what matters most.	Appealing to learner's strengths will allow him or her to see important information in a way that best suits him or her.
...become aware of their own ways of learning so they can better examine and manage their energies and efforts.	All of the models discussed in this book can be applied here.
...find a balance of intellectual contests and academic support.	Students can be challenged to take more risks when they are armed with the "support" of their academic identity.
...become unambiguously aware of their principles, beliefs, preconceptions, and prior learning— and are willing to unlearn when required.	Knowing each student as a type of learner opens the door to connect on a more personal basis. Taking the time to discover how each student can be most successful will show him or her the level of care you have for them individually.
...connect new information to prior understanding.	Students should demonstrate their background knowledge of a topic within their learning preference first, before adding new content.
...organize what they are learning in personally significant, academically appropriate ways.	Enabling students to use their VARK mode(s) to show what they know inherently makes the content more personal and meaningful.
...seek and find real-world purpose for what they are learning.	Kinesthetic learners especially will appreciate seeing how they can use knowledge in real life.

Students learn more when they...	Application to VARK
...are assessed and evaluated on what matters most and understand the decisive factors against which they will be judged.	Assessment is absolutely necessary for instructors to know if the student has met the necessary objectives. However, the way that students are assessed and evaluated can and should differ by learning mode.
...work regularly and constructively with instructors.	Establishing a personal interest in how students can be most successful (not just in your classroom, but as life-long learners) makes them more likely to cooperate with you in return.
...work steadily and productively with other students.	When every student is supported to use his or her strengths to learn, he or she will approach work with a new confidence and be more committed and more productive.
...devote as much time and high-quality effort as possible.	Assessing students based on their preferences gives students a chance to shine using what they know how to do best.

(Angelo 1993)

Sample activities for each learning style

The setting:

A fifth-grade class is learning about the constitution. Their teacher, Miss Kimball, has given them an overview of the United States Constitution, and they have all heard the Preamble lyrics several times using the song from *Schoolhouse Rock!*

······································

Activity #1: Preamble to the U.S. Constitution

Learning preference: Visual

Description: The student will break the Preamble down into chunks or sections of words and make a picture or symbol for each chunk to prompt his or her memory for the next set of words. Suggested "chunking," or division, of the Preamble is: 1) We the people of the United States, 2) in order to form a more perfect Union, 3) establish Justice, 4) insure domestic Tranquility, 5) provide for the common defense, 6) promote the general Welfare, 7) and secure the Blessings of Liberty to ourselves and our Posterity, 8) do ordain and establish this Constitution for the United States of America.

Accommodations for special needs populations:

English language learners: This strategy breaks down the information into simplified divisions and uses pictures to help them remember the next set of words. However, when choosing a picture or symbol, students who are native to the English language will be familiar with *similar* symbols for portions of the text, but ELL's may need to be shown options or examples of appropriate pictures or symbols.

Above-level learners: Challenge these students to find the historical significance of the Preamble and make it relevant for today's society. In addition, they could rewrite the Preamble in their own words and, using a graphic organizer, visually link the parts of their rewritten Preamble to what they think makes a good government.

Below-level learners: These students can practice the Preamble with a partner and can practice reciting it several times before doing so in their final assessment. These learners will also benefit from seeing different examples of pictures and symbols chosen by other learners. This may help them to remember the parts of the Preamble.

Varying instruction methods according to grade level:

Elementary level: Elementary students can make flip charts of the vocabulary used in the Preamble before attempting this activity. They can also be given only one division per small group and asked to draw part of a mural depicting the entire Preamble.

Intermediate level: Challenge these visual students to use photography to capture images that represent the different sections of the Preamble. They could use these photos to create advertisements for the Constitution based on the Preamble.

Secondary level: Visual learners at this level can create a QuickTime® movie that includes various media (audio, visual, digital, and print) to interpret what portions of the Preamble mean and also to emphasize the significance of this document to citizens today.

Activity #2: U.S. Bill of Rights

Learning preference: Aural

Description: The student will be able to describe the first 10 amendments to the U.S. Constitution, also known as the Bill of Rights. After a whole-class discussion about the meaning of each of the 10 amendments, students will participate in an aural presentation on the importance of one of the first 10 amendments.

Accommodations for special needs populations:

English language learners: It is essential that English language learners be paired with strong partners to actively participate in a Think-Pair-Share activity. In a Think-Pair-Share activity, there are three distinct steps:

1. Think: The teacher poses the task or challenge and gives time for each student to think about it on his or her own,

2. Pair: Students are grouped in pairs to discuss their thoughts. In this activity, they could be grouped based on similarly chosen amendments.

3. Share: Student pairs share their ideas with the whole class. These learners should feel comfortable in this activity, because it focuses on oral communication and they are only breaking down the details of one amendment versus all 10 at once. They will also benefit from seeing the examples acted out by other students for deeper understanding of other amendments.

Above-level learners: Ask these students to research the reason that these amendments were made to the Constitution in the first place and give a brief oral presentation to the class.

Below-level learners: Ask these students to use graphic organizers during the Think-Pair-Share activity to organize their thoughts during discussion. For below-level aural learners, provide an audio file or short video that allows them to listen to each of the first 10 amendments before having them work with partners during the Think-Pair-Share activity. Most of these learners would rather present the information to the class by themselves.

Varying instruction methods according to grade level:

Elementary level: Present various jingles or mnemonics for aural learners, many of which are available online, to help students remember the 10 different amendments; or challenge these aural learners to create their own jingles in the skit for the amendment that they choose to feature in the skit.

Intermediate level: Middle-level aural students could come up with clues, jingles, and/or short stories for each of the first 10 amendments, as well as research the facts that answer questions about the "who," "what," and "where" of the Bill of Rights. Each student could have his or her own bingo card with names, dates, locations, and amendments one through 10 written in the bingo boxes. As clues are read, students place a chip on the square that best fits the description given to earn a bingo.

Secondary level: High school-level aural students could participate in a Think-Pair-Share activity about one of the rights they would not want to change at home or at school. In this activity, each student pair could act out or develop a story about that right and what life would be like *without* it. Then they present these scenarios for the class to try to guess which right the student is referencing.

Activity #3: Focus on the U.S. Constitution

Learning preference: Read-Write

Description: The student will be able to describe the significance of the U.S. Constitution. Students will compare and contrast the role of the Constitution of the United States of America in both past and present-day society.

Accommodations for special needs populations:

English language learners: These students should first be supplied with a list of some of the vocabulary terms and meanings that are presented in a whole-class overview of the Constitution. They can use this list as they do research for any of these projects.

Above-level learners: Ask these students to write about the principles of the U.S. Constitution in terms of civil liberties during times of warfare. These students can compose persuasive essays or participate in an open debate on the issue of placing Japanese-Americans in internment camps during World War II and make comparisons to any analogous practices in today's society.

Below-level learners: These learners can use Venn diagrams to guide their writing and to compare the rights of citizens in the 18th century to those in present day.

Varying instruction methods according to grade level:

Elementary level: These students would enjoy a book called *The 500 Hats of Bartholomew Cubbins* (Seuss 1938). In this book, a young boy goes to town to sell his cranberries and has to face an angry king in the palace. The king is angry because Bartholomew does not remove his hat when the king goes by. Each time Bartholomew tries to remove it, another hat appears in its place. The king wants to punish him. Elementary students could write a letter to Bartholomew telling him of his rights and freedoms. Or, they could write about one of the king's rules and tell how the kingdom would be different without that rule. They could also compare the king's rule to a part of the U.S. Constitution in the same manner.

Intermediate level: These students can work with three or four others in a team to complete a class Constitution Timeline Scavenger Hunt, solving clues by researching facts about and applications of the Constitution through history.

Secondary level: These students can research the Constitution of another country, such as Croatia, and write a comparison of that country's core values versus those depicted in the U.S. Constitution.

Activity #4: United States' Founding Fathers Skits

Learning preference: Kinesthetic

Description: The student will actively demonstrate his or her understanding of the roles of some of the Founding Fathers.

Accommodations for special needs populations:

English language learners: Each student chooses a Founding Father, then identifies three main questions about this person and writes the questions in the left column of a double-entry journal. As the student finds out more information, he or she writes the answers in the right column. Once the research is done, the student can create a mobile with pictures or objects that symbolize the facts that he or she found about the chosen person.

Above-level learners: Ask these students to compare the views of their chosen Founding Father to one of today's political leaders.

Below-level learners: Provide these students with a flip chart, index cards, or other graphic organizers to help find essential information about their chosen Founding Fathers. These students will appreciate having resource materials or websites readily available for each Founding Father that can provide a guide to help them get started on their projects right away instead of spending time on random Internet searches.

Varying instruction methods according to grade level:

Elementary level: Play Pin the Fact on the Founder. These students could work in small groups to prepare sets of three facts about each Founding Father in small groups. Each fact should be put on a separate piece of paper. Place pictures and names of the Founding Fathers on a bulletin board and then review them by mixing up the facts and having the students pin the correct fact onto the correct picture.

Intermediate level: Middle-level kinesthetic students can create a video, *Microsoft Powerpoint*® presentation, bulletin board, or collage about their chosen Founding Father.

Secondary level: Demonstrate the views of a Founding Father by participating in a mock question-and-answer session with the press. Students can prepare for the press conference ahead of time by developing the questions and answers in addition to rehearsing their roles. These skits can be videotaped and used for review, as well.

Teachers and parents working together to accommodate these learning styles

The first step for parents is to understand the differences between each of the learning modes assessed by the VARK questionnaire. Once they understand the VARK preferences, then the applications for studying and preparing for exams will be helpful tools to use at home. Please refer parents to or supply them with the tables after this section for more in-depth study tips and exam preparation methods.

If a student's preference is Visual, then he or she will prefer to always have a visual aid present during any presentation, lecture, or study session. This student learns best through videos, interactive websites, diagrams, and flow charts. This student may prefer to study alone in a quiet room.

If a student's preference is Aural, then he or she needs to hear a lesson aloud in order to really absorb the information. This person may find it hard to read silently. After class, he or she may need to reread the information again aloud to actually retain it. Group discussions work well for this type of learner, and it may be a good idea for this person to record lectures or listen to podcasts to use later for studying.

If a student's preference is Reading-Writing, he or she will prefer to have information presented visually and in a written language format. This student works well when the teacher presents important information in an organized format. This type of learner excels by using color-coded notes and study sheets marked with highlighters.

If a student's preference is Kinesthetic, then he or she is a real "hands-on" learner who does not like to be stuck in a classroom listening to a lecture. This student likes to be a part of a demonstration, outdoor field study, and lab work. He or she would much rather "do" than "sit and get." It is important for this student to sit in the front of a classroom to help pay attention when a teacher does need to lecture (Morgan 2008).

How to offer home support

Visual mode	Aural mode
• Reconstruct images in different ways to try different spatial arrangements. • Redraw pages from memory. • Replace words with symbols or initials. **For exams:** • Recall the pictures of pages. • Draw or use diagrams where appropriate. • Write exam answers. • Practice turning your visuals back into words.	• Expand notes by talking with others and collecting notes from the textbook. • Record notes verbally in an MP3 file. • Ask others to hear your interpretation of a topic. • Read notes aloud to yourself. • Explain your notes to another aural person. **For exams:** • Talk with the examiner. • Transcribe your recorded notes. • Spend time in quiet places recalling the ideas. • Practice writing answers to old exam questions. • Speak the answers.
Read-Write mode	**Kinesthetic mode**
• Write out the words again and again. • Read your notes (silently) again and again. • Rewrite the ideas and principles. • Organize any diagrams or graphs into statements, e.g., "The trend is…" • Turn reactions, actions, charts, and flows into words. • Imagine your lists arranged in multichoice questions and distinguish each from the other. **For exams:** • Write out exam answers. • Practice with multiple-choice questions. • Write paragraph beginnings and endings. • Write your thoughts as lists (a, b, c, d, or 1, 2, 3, 4). • Arrange your ideas into hierarchies and points.	• Your lecture notes may be poor because the topics were not concrete or relevant. • You will remember the real things that happened. • Put plenty of examples into your summary. • Use case studies and applications to help with principles and abstract concepts. • Talk about your notes with others. • Use pictures and photographs that illustrate an idea. • Go back to the laboratory or your lab manual. • Recall the experiments or field trip. **For exams:** • Write practice answers and paragraphs. • Role play the exam situation in your own room.

 *Conclusion*

As an extension to learning Newton's laws of motion, Mr. Brook's physics class is studying the cartoon laws of physics. After reviewing short segments of cartoons with The Road Runner, Bugs Bunny, and other characters (Looney Tunes 1948) his students are to list a new set of the laws of motion as they apply to the motion of cartoon characters and compare and contrast them to Newton's laws of motion. Mr. Brook explained that the compare and contrast portion of the assignment can be demonstrated in many different ways, as chosen by the student, as long as all portions of the rubric they are given are addressed in the project.

 Think about it!

- What is Mr. Brook's VARK preference from what you have read about this project?
- How does this activity appeal to Visual learners? Aural learners? Read-Write learners? Kinesthetic learners?
- What activity or project could be added to incorporate something more for Kinesthetic learners?
- What part of this project will be best remembered during assessments by students in each learning style?
- In what ways can Mr. Brook guide his students to choose projects that best fit their learning styles? Why should he do so?

Chapter 5

Assessing Learning Styles

Description

The theory behind learning styles supports the belief that if a child is taught by targeting his or her learning strengths and preferences, then he or she can learn. Academic testing should not be the issue. A student who is taught in an environment that accommodates preferences and individual abilities should be capable of taking any achievement test that measures knowledge and academic skills and show growth over the course of a school year. This begs the question, "When did test-taking preparation become part of the curriculum?" The stress placed on educators today for students to score well on achievement tests in language arts, math, science, and social studies has led to a new subject: test preparation. Teachers complain that there is not enough time in the day to teach all that needs to be taught. Academic success is tied to teacher accountability, school accountability, No Child Left Behind accountability, school report cards, and funding. If the focus is brought back to curriculum and how teachers deliver the curriculum, then perhaps there might be enough time to teach the basics with academic success, and educational institutions would again be places for learning, not just test-taking.

History

According to prominent experts in the field of brain-based research, up to 70 percent of learning style strengths may be genetic (Gardner 2006; Levine 2006; Thies 2000). Children are born with certain learning strengths, and successful students are those who are encouraged to learn by using those strengths. Research shows there are environmental and developmental influences as children grow and mature (Dunn, Dunn, and Perrin

1994). We don't want children or educators thinking that young brains are "etched in stone" (Scherer 2006) Overwhelming statistical research indicates that matching learning strengths and teaching techniques leads to improved achievement scores, as well as more positive attitudes from children about school and learning.

Experts in the field of learning styles all agree that people learn differently based on their innate abilities and strengths. Understanding these strengths or preferences can assist individuals of all ages to have successful learning experiences throughout their lives. If educators are to address the needs of their students, they need valid and reliable tools with which to determine students' learning styles.

Therefore, it is necessary to look at a variety of tools used to assess and identify individual learning style strengths. When individual learning styles are identified, the learning experience can be adapted to suit a variety of students at many levels. Educators and administrators need to develop an understanding of their individual learning style preferences and then accept and identify the needs of their staff, faculties, and students in order to create a positive atmosphere of engagement in the educational environment.

Learning style assessment and Anthony Gregorc

The instrument

The assessment instrument in Dr. Gregorc's model is titled "The Style Delineator" (Gregorc 1982). It is a self-assessment instrument for adults. "The Style Delineator" is designed to help adults identify and quantify the four combinations of the strongest perceptual and ordering abilities of each individual. There are four categories:

- Concrete Sequential (CS)
- Abstract Random (AR)
- Abstract Sequential (AS)
- Concrete Random (CR)

The assessment is based on a psychologically formulated matrix of 40 descriptive words. It is a self-scoring instrument that is sold in a package that contains directions, the Word Matrix, scoring directions, Style Profile Graphic, Style Comparison Synopsis Chart, and a list of Key Ideas. In addition, the book—*An Adult's Guide to Style* (Gregorc 1986)—is necessary to complete an interpretation and analysis of the Style Delineator.

The instrument and children

Gregorc agrees with other experts that individual learning style profiles are a combination of nature and nurture (Gregorc 1979). He also believes in the alignment between learning and teaching style. However, Gregorc's website (http://www.gregorc.com) clearly states that "a child's or student's CS/AS/AR/CR-based style instrument is not available due to philosophical, ethical, and technical views of Dr. Gregorc" (1999–present). Upon further investigation, Dr. Gregorc states that he will not develop a student or youth instrument and will not give permission to others to develop a student instrument using his CS/AS/AR/CR-based research. He further indicates that through his research—based on his theory—he was unable to determine statistical validity for children during his research. Dr. Gregorc expresses concern for the misuse and harm that a student version of his Style Delineator might cause through misleading results or the inability of younger students to identify personal learning styles through self-analysis.

Although Gregorc admits the value of self-awareness and identifying learning style strengths in adults, his instrument—by his own admission—requires the qualities of an Abstract perceptual preference and a Sequential ordering preference, making the identification of personal learning preferences difficult for adults possessing CR/AR/CS profiles. "The Learning Style Delineator" is a paper-and-pencil instrument that is not geared to multiple learning styles.

The instrument and teaching

According to Gregorc, teaching styles are behaviors, characteristics, and mannerisms that reflect underlying mental qualities used for presenting data in school. In order to understand how their personal mindsets affect individual approaches to classes, choices of teaching methods, media, tests, and environmental classroom arrangements, teachers must understand their personal mind styles. Gregorc's website states that "such knowledge is absolutely necessary for responsive and responsible professional behavior" (1999–present). One of the important considerations for teachers is the redefinition of equal education for all learners. This concept once meant access to buildings, resources, and trained teachers for the disadvantaged, but today, according to Gregorc, it means not delivering the same curriculum in the same manner with the same goals, texts, classrooms, or methodologies to all learners. Rather, the educator must understand student differences and personal learning styles and provide varied methodologies to encompass all learning style preferences (Gregorc 1979).

Learning style assessment and the Dunn and Dunn model

The instrument

The Dunn and Dunn Learning Styles Model emphasizes primary instruction through students' strongest modalities, with support and further reinforcement through secondary strengths and teaching new information through varied creative means (Dunn and Griggs 2003). Drs. Rita and Ken Dunn define learning style as the way in which each learner begins to concentrate on, process, and retain new and difficult information (Dunn, Dunn, and Perrin 1994).

The cornerstone of the learning style theory has been the study of global versus analytic traits, according to Dr. Armin Thies, neuropsychologist from Yale University Medical School. Researchers have consistently demonstrated that the majority of young children are not analytic; most appear to be global processors (Dunn and Dunn 1992). Even at the secondary level, analytics taught analytically and globals taught globally achieved at comparable levels. A number of studies conducted by such researchers as Brennan, Douglas, Dunn, Bruno, Sklar and Beaudry, Orazio, and Trautman (Sullivan 1996), demonstrated that global learners exposed to global instructional techniques and resources scored significantly higher than global children taught with analytic techniques and resources.

The initial assessment tool to determine learning style strengths was a pencil-and-paper instrument called the "Learning Style Instrument" (LSI) (Dunn and Dunn 1978). It was geared to upper elementary through high school students. It was followed by the "Learning Style Questionnaire" (Dunn and Dunn 1978) that was expanded to include kindergarten through second graders. Many human resource departments and institutions of higher education, especially those specializing in the training of new teachers, became aware of learning styles. The instrument "Productivity Environmental Preference Survey" (PEPS) (Dunn, Dunn, and Price 1982) was created to determine adult learning style preferences. An adult was defined as anyone over the age of 18. Concurrently, the "Reading Style Inventory" was created by Dr. Marie Carbo (1988) to combine reading with learning styles.

Dr. Janet Perrin created the "Learning Style Inventory: Primary" (LSI: P) (1981) to determine the learning style strengths of kindergarten through second graders. The problem with all these instruments was revealed as brain theory and neuropsychological research became more sophisticated through modern technology.

It became apparent that if global and analytic children needed congruent learning environments as noted by Burke, Guastello, Dunn, Griggs, Beasley, Gemake, Sinatra, and Lewthwaite (1998), then it was equally important that assessments be designed to accommodate global learners. Previously, when all available instruments were analytic, low scores were consistently reported by Burke et al. (1998) on 10–50 percent of global children. This suggested that the instrument was limited by its sequential format, which favored analytic students. It became apparent that global learners were being penalized with an analytically formatted assessment.

To correct this problem, "Learning Style: The Clue to You!" (LS:CY!) (Burke et al. 1998) was developed with a global format to elicit more accurate responses from global students who comprise the majority at these grade levels.

Since the 1980s, additional learning style instruments have been developed. Rundle and Dunn designed and adapted these same principles for identifying adult learning style preferences. "Building Excellence" (BE) (Rundle and Dunn 1996–2000) is a globally-formatted assessment that replaced the PEPS.

More recently, the LSI for high school students has been replaced with the globally formatted "Learning in Vogue: Elements of Style" (LIVES) (Missere and Dunn 2007). Guastello and Dunn (1998) added "Our Wonderful Learning Styles" (OWLS) as an elementary assessment instrument. The "Observational Preschool/Primary Assessment of Learning Styles" (OPALS) (Nieter and Dunn 2008) extends the learning style instruments available to children as young as three years old.

All of these instruments incorporate stories, colorful illustrations, humor, and attributes that enhance the learning style assessment needs of global learners. Although the instruments are created to meet the needs of global preferences, both analytic learners and those with varied learning styles demonstrated an increase in positive attitude toward the assessments, and no negative effects were evidenced by analytic learners using a global instrument. The opposite was not found to be true.

Use the chart on the following page for a quick view of the different diagnostic instruments available, as well as the processing styles and populations they accommodate.

Instruments responsive to the Dunn and Dunn Learning Styles Model

Instrument	Processing Style	Principal Researcher(s)/Year	Targeted Population
"Learning Style Inventory"	Analytic	Dunn, Dunn, and Price (1985)	Grades 3–12
"Learning Style Questionnaire"	Analytic	Dunn and Dunn (1978)	Grades K–12
"Productivity Environmental Preference Survey"	Analytic	Dunn, Dunn, and Price (1982)	Adults
"Reading Style Inventory"	Analytic	Carbo (1988)	Grades 2–8
"Learning Style Inventory: Primary"	Analytic	Perrin (1981)	Grades K–2
"Building Excellence"	Global	Rundle and Dunn (1996–2000)	Adults
"Our Wonderful Learning Style"	Global	Guastello and Dunn (1998)	Grades 2–5
"Learning Style: The Clue to You!"	Global	Burke et al. (1998)	Grades 6–8
"Learning In Vogue: Elements of Style"	Global	Missere and Dunn (2007)	Grades 9–12
"Elementary Learning Style Assessment"	Global	Dunn, Burke, and Rundle (2007)	Grades 2–5
"Observational Preschool/Primary Assessment of Learning Styles"	Global	Nieter and Dunn (2008)	Grades Preschool–1

The preschool/primary instrument is observational and therefore does not affect the experience for the students. However, its colorful format that matches the five dimensions of the Dunn and Dunn Model (as noted in Chapter 2) makes it user-friendly for teachers who may have more global tendencies.

The instrument and children

The underlying premise of the Dunn and Dunn Model is the concept that all children can learn when their learning style preferences are identified and matched to teaching. All learning style assessments associated with the Dunn and Dunn Model are available online. Children in second grade through adults are able to log on individually or in a computer lab and complete the assessments. The instrument format consists of stories that illustrate the different learning style components and questions about the child's personal preferences, replete with colorful illustrations. When a student completes the assessment, which takes about 20 minutes, a Student Profile is generated along with a Homework Prescription.

The Student Profile identifies a student's strengths and preferences for 20 elements across the five dimensions of the Dunn and Dunn Model (see Chapter 2). It is important to explain individual differences to the students. Self-image and positive learning experiences become the first steps in a worthwhile school experience. When students understand their own learning strengths, learning becomes a self-advocating process and helps develop responsibility in them.

The Homework Prescription is especially useful for explaining to parents how their children learn best. Teachers may be able to lessen a great deal of parent/child friction if, armed with a Homework Prescription, the teacher can explain to the parent why his or her child might actually study more productively with an iPod® and headphones.

Imagine a parent/teacher conference in which a parent does not believe that their child can study or do homework in front of the television, with the stereo blasting, or the computer streaming music videos. If the teacher understands that this child has a high preference for sound, then he or she can explain why this environment might be beneficial for the student. If a student is sprawled on the floor or the bed, his or her preference may be for an informal design. The parent/teacher conference might alleviate the parents' concerns about this preference. If parents understand what a Student Profile determines, then they can establish a more positive learning environment at home that is as supportive as the learning environment in school.

The instrument and teaching

Research acknowledges that while some learning styles are genetic in nature, environmental influences and natural development, as well as growth, can cause changes in student learning profiles over time. Whereas a teacher who is equipped with student learning style profiles can create a positive learning environment, a teacher with no information cannot begin to accommodate individual differences. Some teachers differentiate instruction by alternating methods of learning. As shown in Figure 5.1 below, if a teacher is applying each learning style for only a portion of the day, then a child is learning in his or her strength only 25 percent of the time and not being attended to 75 percent of the time. But with information about preferences, a teacher can create more equitable learning environments that allow students to use their area of strength more frequently.

Figure 5.1 Classroom Activities by Learning Style

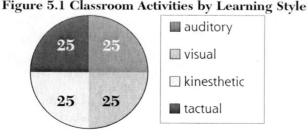

Homework prescriptions are increasingly useful as students proceed through the school system. As departmentalization increases and students encounter many more teachers, they may not always have teachers who are committed to or understand learning styles. If students in high school or institutions of higher learning understand their own learning style preferences, then they can study within their strengths and improve their ability to interpret and understand information.

In a learning style environment, teachers can involve students in creating materials for tactile learners, allow movement for kinesthetic learners, provide informal as well as formal design, and pay attention to lighting or sound preferences. Small-group instruction, individual instruction, and nonconformity issues lessen when identified and attended to.

It is important to note that the traditional learning environment favors analytic learners with strong auditory and visual skills. Most colleges, including teacher-training programs, use the chalk-and-talk, lecture, and note-taking teaching methods. It is not unusual then for teachers to turn around and teach the same way in which they learned. Awareness of differences in strengths, as well as knowing one's own learning profile, goes a long way toward implementing learning styles. Without assessments, it is impossible to identify learning styles and address them or celebrate individuality and differences.

With this information about each student, a teacher can differentiate instruction based on learning style profiles. Opportunities can be created to accommodate a variety of learning styles.

Learning style assessment and Howard Gardner

The instrument

Howard Gardner, much to his chagrin, expects to be known as "The Father of Multiple Intelligences." That is not to belittle in any way the effect his research has had on educating young people since the 1980s. However, in many interviews, writings, and on his own webpage, he states, "I always maintained that I was a psychologist and not an educator, and did not presume to know how best to teach a class or run a school" (Gardner 2006). His research stems from a different orientation, and although he has been an active participant in assisting educators to put his theories into practice, his perspective is different. He states very clearly that learning styles and intelligences are "really fundamentally different psychological constructs" (Gardner 2006).

In response to a request to create a set of measures for educators and parents to ascertain the intellectual profile of young children, Dr. Gardner participated in Project Spectrum. His intent was to design 15 separate tasks that would assess the several intelligences in "as natural a manner as possible" (Gardner 2006). He developed, in cooperation with David Feldman and Mara Krechevsky, the Spectrum Battery. He ultimately determined that he was not interested in the costly and time-consuming business of creating assessments.

Dr. Gardner is further concerned that the creation of a set of tests of each intelligence—"an intelligence-fair version" (2006)—might lead to negative forms of labeling that further stigmatize students. His intent was not to develop a way to categorize students, but rather to help students learn. Therefore, there is no specific instrument that creates a multiple intelligence profile.

Other researchers have developed multiple intelligence (MI) tests. For example, the MIDAS™ test was created by Branton Shearer (1987). Dr. Gardner criticizes these instruments for not actually measuring strengths and presupposing that the test takers possess intrapersonal intelligence or the ability to know themselves well and report on that. The reason he says that these instruments do not measure strengths is because they do not contain a performance task section that would be necessary to determine certain intelligences in his domain. Under the auspices of Project Zero (Harvard Univ. 2010) at Eliot Pearson Children's School at Tufts University in Massachusetts, Project Spectrum (Harvard Univ. 2010) added art portfolios and teachers' observations of children engaged in activities in response to Dr. Gardner's criticisms. The Key School in Indiana further added videotape in their assessment of the learning process.

The instrument and children

Dr. Gardner does not hold standardized high stake tests in great regard. He believes that school grades and class ranking are better predictors, for example, than SAT scores or IQ test scores for success in college. Although there are ways to prepare or practice for these tests, these standardized exams only use a blend of linguistic and logical intelligences. Dr. Gardner's opinion on testing of all kinds is as follows: "I believe that we should get away altogether from tests and correlations among tests, and look instead at more naturalistic sources of information about how peoples around the world develop skills important to their way of life" (Gardner 1987).

The biggest shortcoming of standardized tests is that they require students to show what they have learned in a very specific, predetermined way. Standardized tests ignore all the valuable information that learning styles provide on how students learn best often to the detriment of nontraditional learners.

If teachers want to know and identify their students' strengths, Gardner encourages teachers to take their students to places, such as a children's museum or an enhanced playground with a variety of activities and observe them carefully. Second, he encourages teachers to give students, their parents, and their teachers from the previous year a small questionnaire about their own strengths. He believes that only through corroboration of the three can a teacher be confident about a student's strengths and weaknesses.

The instrument and teaching

Assessing students' multiple intelligences in the classroom is an ongoing process that is heavily based on observation. For authentic assessment in the classroom to have validity, documentation is equally as important. This kind of authentic record keeping requires excellent organizational skills on the part of the teacher and dedication to keeping student portfolios. Initially, deciding on the format for the portfolio and creating a checklist to maintain records of what has been collected on a per student/per learning area basis may seem overwhelming; however, once the skill has been developed, it can be the most rewarding way of assessing students and of developing a wonderful educational experience. Some suggestions for authentic assessment portfolios are included. Please note that not all elements need to be included in each assessment portfolio, since some items will not complement certain strengths while others will highlight them. That is why a portfolio is an accurate way of determining MI strengths in a variety of students.

Portfolios can include the following:

- anecdotal records
- student work samples
- audio recordings of students reading, interviews, singing, or participating in group activities
- videotapes of students acting, giving reports, playing sports, or engaging in nature activities
- photographs that document the year's activities
- student journals
- student charts
- informal tests
- practice versions of standardized tests
- student interviews from conferences
- criterion-referenced assessments (for concrete evaluation) of specific tasks, e.g., can or cannot add two-digit numbers
- checklists
- classroom maps
- calendar records

An understanding of Multiple Intelligences and assessments offers the ability to move away from standardized test practices whether they be state tests, norm-referenced tests, or teacher-created classroom tests. MI, by definition, supports individualized instruction, recognition of individualization among students, and individualizing our assessments. It is not necessary for teachers to reinvent the wheel in an MI classroom. There are a variety of predesigned materials for teachers to use to create authentic assessment within an MI setting. Many of them were created either by researchers who carried on with MI and their practical application in the classroom or with Howard Gardner's input and interest through Harvard's Education Department.

Learning style assessment and Neil D. Fleming

The instrument

Neil Fleming created his version of a Learning Style Assessment questionnaire in 1983. The acronym VARK stands for the four modalities that Fleming addresses in his assessment: Visual, Aural, Read-Write, and Kinesthetic. When asked if VARK is a learning style, he responded that it is not because learning styles have more than 18 multidimensions, including environmental, emotional, sociological, and psychological aspects. VARK deals only with physiological aspects of learning styles, and only the perceptual portion of that aspect. "VARK is about one preference, our preference for taking in and putting out information in a learning context" (Fleming 2001). The theory is that it is possible for people to change this aspect of their learning style, and so it is advantageous to understand and identify our preferences.

Also, the VARK questionnaire is strictly for use in terms of learning, not leisure. Emphasis is placed on the issue that *preferences* are not the same as *strengths*. The VARK questionnaire defines learning style preferences in the domain of perceptual learning.

There are three components to VARK: The standard "VARK" questionnaire, version 7.0 for high school, college, and adult learners, available in a pencil-and-paper version or, since 2001, in an online version available at http://www.vark-learn.com, in 25 different languages; the "VARK questionnaire for younger people" is a 16-item questionnaire created for younger people ages 12–18 that parallels the adult version with questions more suitable to the age group and was updated to its current format in 2007; and an "Athletes VARK questionnaire" for use with coaches and educators working with high school, college, and adult athletes.

VARK can be administered to a class, group, or team. It can be used in a one-to-one training or counseling situation, as well. The person taking the questionnaire is instructed either orally or in print to pick the best answer to each of 16 questions. They are permitted to pick two answers for a particular question if they feel that is a more appropriate response. They then submit the answers online and receive a profile of their preferences, but not necessarily their strengths. It is possible to score the questionnaires by hand if an institution uses the printed pencil-and-paper version of the assessment. Otherwise, it is scored as soon as one clicks the OK button on the computer at the end of the questionnaire.

The instrument and children

The VARK questionnaire does not directly apply to young children because it is necessary to be able to read and choose reflectively among several choices. To be effective it requires a degree of maturity to self-analyze one's own preferences. Inasmuch as it is used for those studying to become teachers and to create sensitivity to differences in learning preferences, it does affect how children may be perceived and taught by their teachers. As students enter middle and high school, the "VARK questionnaire for younger people" can be used to identify learning preferences in the perceptual modalities. It adds a level of understanding that everyone is not the same and that just because one learns differently it does not mean that he or she is not smart.

When the questionnaire is completed and submitted, the resulting profile is delivered online as Helpsheets, which teach the student how to interpret the results and determine what strategies to use to maximize learning. There is a description of preferences for taking in information, a segment labeled "SWOT," or "Study WithOut Tears," which offers study techniques specific to that learning preference, as well as advice for how to use this knowledge before an exam. The Helpsheets are created to assist the learner to understand his or her preferences and develop additional, effective strategies for learning and improving communication skills (VARK 2001). The charts below and on the following pages demonstrate the kind of information provided by these Helpsheets for Aural, Visual, Read-Write, and Kinesthetic learners.

Aural study strategies

Take in information:	"Study WithOut Tears":	Prepare for an assignment or exam:
• attend classes • attend discussions and tutorials • discuss topics with others or your teachers • explain ideas to others • use a recording device • focus on examples, stories, and jokes • describe the overheads, pictures, and visuals to another person • leave spaces in your notes for later recall	• convert or expand your notes by talking with others and collecting additional information from the textbook • summarize notes onto recordings and listen to them • ask others to listen to your explanation of a topic • read your summarized notes aloud	• imagine talking with the examiner • listen to your inner dialogue and write down your thoughts • spend time in a quiet place recalling the ideas • practice writing answers to old exam questions • speak your answers aloud or silently inside your head

Read-Write study strategies

Take in information:	"Study WithOut Tears":	Prepare for an assignment or exam:
• make lists • use headings • use dictionaries, glossaries, definitions • use handouts • use textbooks • take notes and reread them often • practice writing essays • use manuals (computing and laboratory)	• convert your notes into summaries or rewrite them • reread your notes • rewrite ideas and principles • describe any graphs as statements (e.g., "the trend is...") • describe diagrams, charts, and flows with words • imagine lists arranged as multiple-choice questions	• write exam answers • practice with multiple-choice questions • write paragraph beginnings and endings • number your ideas as lists • arrange your words into hierarchies and points

Visual study strategies

Take in information:	"Study WithOut Tears":	Prepare for an assignment or exam:
• pay attention to gestures and descriptive language • use visuals such as pictures, videos, and slides • look for flowcharts, diagrams, and graphs in texts	• underline text with different colored highlighters • reconstruct images in different ways or spatial arrangements • replace words with symbols or initials • convert lecture notes into pictures	• make drawings or diagrams • recall the pictures you created • practice turning your visual back into words

Kinesthetic study strategies

Take in information:	"Study WithOut Tears":	Prepare for an assignment or exam:
<ul><li>use all your senses</li><li>use laboratories</li><li>attend field trips, tours, exhibits</li><li>observe examples of principles</li><li>ask lecturers for real-life examples</li><li>practice with hands-on applications and trial and error</li><li>make collections (e.g., rock types, plants, shells, grasses)</li><li>see samples or photographs</li><li>study previous exam papers</li></ul>	<ul><li>remember the "real" things that happened</li><li>use examples in your summaries</li><li>read case studies about abstract concepts</li><li>talk about your notes with another person</li><li>use pictures and photographs</li><li>return to the laboratory or your manual to aid recall</li></ul>	<ul><li>write practice answers and paragraphs</li><li>role-play the exam situation in a quiet place</li></ul>

The instrument and teaching

VARK is offered for wide use in educational research, practical applications, and institutions of higher learning. For those teachers and practioners who have not experienced learning styles, it is a valuable tool. It raises awareness of and sensitivity to the concept that learning is not a one-size-fits-all process and that understanding different preferences, as well as strengths, can assist teachers in creating friendly, supportive learning environments. The VARK website clearly states to teachers that their VARK scores indicate how they learn, but not necessarily how they teach. It will, however, raise awareness that can lead to more effective teaching techniques that include differentiation to accommodate various learning styles.

Because VARK only addresses the perceptual modalities, its influence is limited in terms of a well-rounded learning style profile. Also, until very recently, the scoring and validity of VARK have only been arithmetic and not statistical. As such, it was only applicable as an educational tool. In February 2009, the website updated new statistical information to allow use of VARK for research purposes, adding statistical validity in addition to its initial scoring for identification purposes.

Conclusion

Should we assess learning styles? Should educators understand the different ways in which students gain information? Do educators need an understanding of their own learning styles in relation to how they teach others? The resounding answer to these questions is, "Yes, Yes, Yes!" Differentiated instruction is a high priority in many districts across the nation in an effort to increase student success. Many times in the history of education, a buzzword enters the lexicon, everyone jumps on board, everyone buys flashy new curriculums, and then this fad fizzles out and a new fad explodes on the scene. Research has demonstrated that students learn differently. The curriculum is not the issue. All children need to learn to read, write, think critically, and explore their environment. Children are born curious and have an amazing capacity for learning—but not all learn in the same way. I once heard a colleague complaining about *Sesame Street* (PBS) on public television, "If this administration thinks I am going to put on a bright yellow suit and sing and dance to get these kids' attention, then they better think again!" Education is not about showmanship. Education is about sensitivity, understanding, and creativity.

Children come to school with a million questions. They come to school with wide-eyed wonderment and amazement at the world around them. It is the job of educators to foster that sense of learning, create an environment that encourages questions and answer-seeking, and develop skills that will set children on a path to understanding, critical thinking, and successful learning. The first step is to provide teachers with the tools they need to address individuality within their classrooms. When children learn, they can apply what they learn to any standardized tests. When teachers help children understand that each of them learns differently, children begin with a feeling of safety rather than a feeling of insecurity. First, they need to learn, discover, question, and think. With learning style assessments, teachers can begin to take the first steps towards achieving our nation's educational goals of academic success and prepare our children for what lies ahead.

Think about it!

- Which assessments will you give to students at the beginning of the year?
- How will the results of the assessments impact your room arrangement and your seating chart?
- Revisit your first few weeks of lesson plans. Armed with new knowledge from the learning style assessments, how might you modify or alter your instruction to be more accommodating to the students you are teaching?

Chapter 6

The Yes I Can! Model of Organizing Teaching Within These Learning Styles

Description

Now that you have read through the previous chapters describing the learning style models of some of the groundbreaking researchers in this field, you may be thinking, "How can I put all of this research and knowledge into practice in my own classroom?" This is the point at which many educators throw their hands up and say, "I have too many restrictions with state assessments and No Child Left Behind to worry about trying to incorporate learning style models into my daily teaching routine." We fully believe today's teachers must know each individual student on a personal level and incorporate learning activities tailored to each student's individual needs and learning styles to achieve success. We have developed a model to incorporate learning styles and differentiated instruction to do just that. Using the knowledge gained throughout our learning style research journey, we have incorporated much of the research mentioned in the previous chapters into a practical, working model that can be applied to all disciplines and grade levels. We have worked with educators across the United States to develop this model in their classrooms, and the success has been unequivocal.

History

The Yes I Can! Model: Individualized instruction with technology integration

The Yes I Can! Model (Allen and Scheve 2008) encompasses a differentiated style of instruction that incorporates and integrates standards-based indicators, technology, and individualized learning plans according to individual learning styles. The Yes I Can! Model includes ways to assess student's individual learning styles and to develop individualized learning plans for each student.

The Yes I Can! Model provides a consistent, manageable method of differentiating and individualizing curriculum based on learning styles. However, before discussing this model, here are a few questions to ponder:

- Do I know what my own learning style is?
- Do I know the learning styles of each of my students?
- Do my students know what their learning styles are?
- Do my students have a choice in their work on a daily basis?
- Do I give my students choices based on their learning styles?
- Do I always seek ways to implement technology in my lessons?

In 2004–2005, we were challenged to find a way to individualize and personalize the science curriculum for our students. That challenge led us to draw on more than 25 years of combined teaching experience to develop a system of individualized learning plans called The Yes I Can! Model. This model has since been taught to educators of all disciplines and ages.

The educational reform that we are currently undergoing involves changing the classroom from one that is teacher-centered to student-centered. The ideas that the teacher should be the provider of all knowledge and that the students must simply learn

146

that information in one way are now deemed archaic. Educators have known for many years that students learn by different means, but we are finally beginning to change the way we teach and use these different learning styles.

To individualize learning for students, we allowed them to choose the activities that they wanted to do to reinforce the lesson content. The activities used current technological applications and were tailored to students' individual learning styles.

Once students knew how they learned best, the strategy had a ripple effect. We began to hear our students talk about their other classes in terms of their personal learning styles. They approached their other classes equipped with a new tool, knowing what they could do for themselves to be successful in all content areas.

We live in a world of customization. Our students' education should be the same. We know that each student learns in a different way, but how do we put that philosophy into everyday action and make it an integral part of their learning? The Yes I Can! Model is an interactive multimedia system that can show you how to design a curriculum that is self-directed and outcomes-based. This approach utilizes each student's learning style on a daily basis to ultimately master the indicators at the local, state, and national levels. The advantages do not end at improved test scores. Your students will be practicing indispensable workplace, decision-making, and team-building skills.

The initial Yes I Can! Model learning plans were used for grades 7–12 science courses with an integrated curriculum (life, Earth, and physical sciences). In addition, a great deal of choice for the students involved hands-on interaction with technology in various forms. The curriculum was already standards-based and aligned with state and national standards. The Individualized Learning Plans (ILPs) were based on six student learning styles from which students would make project choices within their top learning styles. As a result of this individualized curriculum, the 2005 State Science Assessment scores were better than ever before at Anderson County High School in Garnett, Kansas, as they met the State Standard of Excellence in Science for the first time.

The accompanying graph (Figure 6.1 below) demonstrates the amount of improvement seen on the State Science Assessment from 2003 to 2005 in 10th-grade science at Anderson County Junior and Senior High School, and in 2008 to 10th- and 11th-graders in the same school. The Kansas Science Assessment was not given in 2004.

Figure 6.1 Improvement on State Science Assessments from 2003–2005

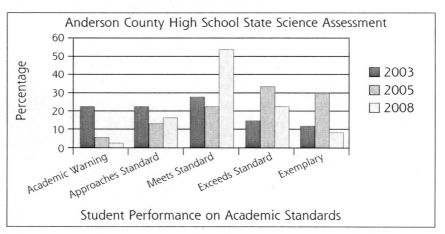

In addition to the individual categories of mastery for each assessment year for science at Anderson County High School, the total level of mastery from all three years of state science assessments at this school showed improvement as well, as seen in Figure 6.2 below.

Figure 6.2 Student Achievement Levels Before and After Implementation of The Yes I Can! Model Learning Plan System

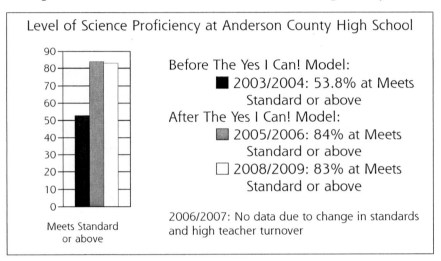

The Yes I Can! Model learning plan system was implemented at this school in 2004. There was a 30.2 percent increase in the level of mastery between the 2003 and 2005 state assessments. In the fall of 2007, this high school experienced a high turnover of teachers within the science department. Out of three high school teachers, only one remained from the previous year. That teacher trained the new arrivals on The Yes I Can! Model learning plan system. Despite the shift in teachers and a change that required *multiple* indicators to be taught (the Kansas State Board made changes to science standards as late as October of 2007), the 2008 testing results excelled with 83 percent at mastery or above, a testament to the effectiveness of The Yes I Can! Model learning plan system.

The Yes I Can! Model of differentiated instruction allows for individualization, assessment, and remediation lessons that are all aligned with state standards. The Individualized Learning Plan consists of both whole-group and individual activities, and offers choices of activities for each student that are tailored to his or her individual learning style. This model has proven successful in mastering standards-based indicators and preparing students of all ages and disciplines for our technology-driven society. The Yes I Can! Model advantage will have an impact on your students, school, and community by igniting a new passion for learning and by instilling a new educational identity for all students!

The Yes I Can! Model five-step implementation process

1. Introduce learning styles

Choose the multiple learning styles that you want to identify for your individualized system. The Yes I Can! Model system makes use of six: Visual, Expressive, Kinesthetic, Auditory, Group, and Individual. (See Figure 6.3 on the following page.) We introduce these learning styles through a *Microsoft PowerPoint*® presentation that describes each type of learning style to students after the survey is taken. This introduction is done on the first day of school.

Figure 6.3 Six Learning Styles for The Yes I Can! Model

Visual
Learn by sight, mainly by reading and writing
Tend to be fast thinkers, gesture while talking, and communicate clearly
Learn from demonstration—must see it to understand
Do better with numbers when they see them written

Auditory
Learn best by listening
Usually need a quiet place
Better with numbers when they can hear them spoken
Has good comprehension when listening to a speaker

Group
Learn best by interacting with others
May attend a study group or form one of their own
First impulse is to socialize instead of finding out what tasks need to be completed

Kinesthetic
Feeling and touch oriented
Good at hands-on tasks
Sensitive to others' feelings
Learn best by moving and doing
Has difficulty sitting for long periods of time

Expressive
Usually does well in speech or writing assignments
Likes to organize thoughts with study cards, highlighting text, and/or reciting aloud while studying
Very comfortable with conveying thoughts either by talking or writing

Individual
Prefer to study alone
Work one-on-one with a peer tutor rather than in a study group
Need a quiet place
Class attendance is crucial

For best results, introduce the learning styles as early in the school year as possible. Set the tone and expectations for the individualized instruction early so the system is not seen as "something new" that is just an experiment. The more specific the instructor is with expectations about the individualized learning system, the more efficient the system will be.

2. Learning style survey

Conduct a learning style survey to assess the types of learners your students represent. Many premade surveys do not specifically match one's grade level or program. Check with your school counselor or administrator to see if all incoming students are given a learning style survey, as some schools conduct a schoolwide survey.

We recommend generating your own learning style survey that specifically relates to your grade level. We used ideas from a vast array of available online surveys and developed our own. The benefit of developing your own survey is that it provides additional personalization. The Yes I Can! Model learning style survey we used is included in Appendix 6.1, pages 161–163.

Conduct the survey the first few days of school to set the tone for individualization from the beginning of the school year. To implement an individualized learning program midway through the school year, you must still give the survey to assess how your students learn best.

Make sure the survey identifies the types of learning styles you have decided to incorporate into your individualized classroom. Remind students to take this survey seriously, as it will set the pace for the rest of the year in terms of how they learn best. Give the students ample time to complete the survey. Get to know your students on a more advanced level by having personal conversations about the results.

Ask the students if they indeed learn best in the style identified by the survey. For example, "Joe, this survey said that you learn best by reading the material, rather than hearing the material. Did that surprise you?" or "Susan, the survey results say you work better in groups than by yourself. Do you think that is true of your learning style?"

Again, gauge these conversations according to grade level, but be sure to have some sort of personal conversation after the survey and results have been calculated to get the responses of students.

After the student works within his or her identified learning styles for a designated period, ask if the student feels that this is the way he or she really learns best. Then have the student redo the survey and make any necessary adjustments.

3. Learning plan development

This is the most time consuming aspect of the The Yes I Can! Model program. The Individual Learning Plan (ILP) must align with learning styles, state standards, indicators, district learning goals, objectives, etc. If the curricular material does not align with the state standard or indicator, then it should not be used. Refer to the template provided in Appendix 6.3, page 168, to understand the elements of the ILP.

Each Individual Learning Plan covers a particular indicator or, in some cases, a group of similar indicators. We call this time frame a Unit. So in essence, the Unit consists of material that pertains to those particular indicator(s). The initial plan development is lengthy. But once you have a draft, you can make adjustments as needed.

To create these plans, we used simple *Microsoft Word*® documents that can be easily modified as needed. Including at least two activities for each learning style ensures that the student has a choice. This means he or she will be more motivated to complete the activity and do a respectable job, since the assignment wasn't forced upon him or her by the teacher. If working with a team or coworker, remember to work smarter, not harder; divide and conquer the plans. Have one teacher develop one plan for a specific indicator while the other develops a plan for another indicator. Once the teacher determines the learning styles of students, activities are then aligned with those learning styles with a variety of different activities for each particular learning style.

4. The plan in action

Students work within one of the top two learning styles identified for them at the beginning of the school year. Each day, try to conduct whole-class activities that consist of *Microsoft PowerPoint*® presentation lectures, small video clips, whole-class review activities such as *Jeopardy!*® games, interactive quizzes, etc. The "whole-group" element varies from 10–20 minutes total.

After whole-group instruction, students break up and begin their individual learning activities listed on the ILP. Keep in mind that this should be a smooth transition.

In our experience, students are anxious to start their individual work time and do not waste time in the transition from whole group to individual work. In fact, many times students request more individual work time. Students choose the activities that they want to do from the list on the ILP.

A sample ILP for a learner with strong Visual and Group preferences is shown in Appendix 6.2, pages 164–167, based on a unit on cells and on a classroom environment lesson.

It makes sense then that an additional advantage of The Yes I Can! Model individualized learning system is classroom management. Behavior problems are minimal because students are actively engaged in learning activities throughout the entire class period.

The system is self-paced so teachers do not waste precious teaching time while waiting for all students to finish one learning activity before beginning another. Once students finish an activity, the teacher checks the student work and provides immediate feedback about the quality of the work. Our students were trained to move on to the next activity of their choice to avoid "down time" as we progressed around the room to sign off on activities.

What is meant by the statement "students were trained" is that students were taught to maintain several classroom expectations during individual work time—not unlike the procedures one has for lining up, signing of hall passes at appropriate times, collecting and distributing work, etc. We established such procedures for individual work time.

Figure 6.4 below shows a sample of five procedures that we established for individual work time. These procedures were practiced each day during the first few weeks of class. The teacher led sessions with the students to illustrate positive examples of individual work time. Once these standards were established, only minimal reminders were needed for students to remain on task.

Figure 6.4 Individual Work Time Procedures

- Raise your hand to signal that you need the teacher.
- Show respect to those working around you by remaining at your workstation and speaking at an appropriate level for the activity.
- Your project deserves all of your attention.
- Keep moving forward. When you finish a project, move on to the next.
- If you need to go get something, go to the bathroom, etc., follow school procedure to leave the classroom. Avoid disrupting others.

Keep in mind that you have set an expectation that students will be continually working and making progress. Hold them to that expectation because in real life, their workplace will make the same demands! In addition, a well-organized plan will assist you and the students to move through the plan with efficiency. By training students to be self-sufficient, self-directed learners, you have built in the time to work with each student individually and can provide each with more personal attention.

Behavior issues are minimal because students are choosing from a variety of interesting, technology-driven, engaging activities that are tailored to how they learn best. Since students get the opportunity to choose which activities they want to do, they take ownership of their educational opportunities. They take on the responsibility of achieving academic success, since they were given a choice.

Once a student completes an activity, he or she calls on the teacher to check the work, and the instructor carries out a small question and answer session. If the work is completed to the teacher's satisfaction, then the allotted points given will be recorded on the student's ILP. The ILP is the only record of these point values, so it is crucial that the student not lose the ILP.

Once students complete an activity and have their work checked, they quickly go to the next learning activity. There is no "one and done" mentality with The Yes I Can! Model individualized learning system. The individual work time is continual with no breaks occurring between completing of one activity and the next. This practice must be managed effectively by the instructor to ensure that the continual learning activities are occuring.

We provide folders for each student to store their ILP, progress logs, and other materials. For example, inside the front cover, students can paste the Learning Styles Product Options Chart. Then, the first page of their portfolio can be their ILP with the baseline activities and assessment tables. These documents never leave the classroom. Provide a place for these folders so students know where to go to retrieve them.

Students work on their chosen activities each day during individual work time and are given points for each successfully completed activity. Rubrics are often provided by the teacher for projects such as posters, videos, skits, and so on.

The time spent on completing the ILP for the specified indicator varies from unit to unit. The indicators vary in terms of difficulty and complexity, so the time spent on each ILP must also be flexible.

Leave the last 10 minutes or so at the end of the class period open for a review or wrap-up of the day's learning activities. Allow students to share what they learned from carrying out their specific individual activities. This provides crucial feedback to the instructor and serves as an informal assessment opportunity. The wrap-up and review session also encourages students to take their individual activities seriously since they must share what they learned with their peers. This practice emphasizes the importance of the individual work time and increases the accountability of the students.

5. Assessment
For the student

Multiple forms of assessment are carried out throughout each unit. Both informal and formal assessment types are conducted daily during whole-group and individual work time. The formal assessments are similar to the state assessment. The question types on the formal assessment are primarily multiple-choice with additional questions as needed. Additional items may be short answer, graphical interpretations, fill-in, essay, etc.

Informal assessment methods include interactive quizzes, teacher-student question-answer sessions, review games, frequent work checks, etc. Formal assessment progress is tracked on the student's Individual Standard Log. The students can paste the Individual Standard Log on the back cover of their portfolios so they can keep track of their progress, as well as provide a means for the teacher to monitor their mastery of standards. (See Appendix 6.4, page 170, for a template of these logs.)

For the teacher

Teachers using this organizational model most often find themselves achieving a level of mastery that lets them feel comfortable with their students, which encourages student feedback. This feedback is used to assess themselves on the organization and implementation of the Yes I Can! Model learning plan system on a daily basis, the level of appropriateness of activities that were offered to learners, and to solicit suggestions or changes that the students have for any part of the system whether it be grading, learning plans, structure, or expectations.

For example, one student suggested that everyone in class keep notebook paper in their personal folders for notetaking so that class time would not be wasted looking for a notebook. Such feedback is essential to improve use of ILPs within the classroom, of course, but also for the development of a trusted relationship between the student and teacher. When a teacher truly values what the students suggest, these students are true members and have a voice. This invokes a sense of ownership for the learning that takes place in this type of classroom.

Assessments are embedded throughout The Yes I Can! Model learning plan system unit as continuous and routine. The formal assessments occur at set times throughout the unit and are recorded in the assessment table of the ILP. The final assessment at the end of the unit is much like a typical teaching sequence. Results from the formal assessments are compiled and used as a tool to direct future course planning. If the overall assessment results are poor, then reteaching of the material is necessary in order for the students to master the indicator of study.

The formal and informal assessment results guide classroom lesson planning and also indicate possible success rate on the state assessments. This informational data is vital to instructors to ensure proper instructional planning for student success and high achievement.

 *Conclusion*

This individualized and differentiated instructional model will empower teachers to say "Yes I Can!" as they:

- identify student learning styles.
- individualize curriculum tailored to individual learning styles.
- integrate technology into the curriculum on a daily basis.
- improve standardized test scores.
- increase overall student success.

 Think about it!

- How can you make sure to accommodate the many learning styles of your students?
- Are there changes you will need to make to your room arrangement, materials, or procedures to engage a wider variety of learning styles?
- Why is it helpful for a student to know his or her own learning style before taking a standardized test?

The Yes I Can! Model Learning Style Survey

The statements below describe various methods of learning. Please answer the following questions on a scale of 1 to 4. A 1 is least indicative of your learning style, and a 4 indicates that the statement correlates to how you learn best.

least indicative ➞ most indicative

1. Making things for my studies helps me to remember what I have learned.	1	2	3	4
2. When I really want to understand what I have read, I read it softly to myself.	1	2	3	4
3. I get more done when I work alone.	1	2	3	4
4. I remember what I have read better than what I have heard.	1	2	3	4
5. When I answer questions, I can say the answer better than write it.	1	2	3	4
6. I enjoy joining in on class discussions.	1	2	3	4
7. I understand math problems better when they are written down rather than heard.	1	2	3	4
8. I understand spoken directions better than written ones.	1	2	3	4
9. I like to work by myself.	1	2	3	4
10. I would rather show and explain how something works than write about how it works.	1	2	3	4
11. If someone tells me three numbers to add, I usually get the right answer without writing them down.	1	2	3	4
12. I prefer to work with a group rather than alone.	1	2	3	4
13. A graph or chart is easier for me to understand than hearing the data.	1	2	3	4

least indicative → most indicative

14. Writing a spelling word several times helps me to remember it better.	1	2	3	4
15. I learn better if someone reads to me rather than reading silently to myself.	1	2	3	4
16. I learn best when I study alone.	1	2	3	4
17. I do my best work in groups.	1	2	3	4
18. In a group project, I would rather make a chart or poster than gather information.	1	2	3	4
19. I remember more of what I learn if I learn it alone.	1	2	3	4
20. I do well in classes where most of the information must be read.	1	2	3	4
21. If I have to decide something, I ask other people for their opinion.	1	2	3	4
22. I like to make things with my hands.	1	2	3	4
23. I don't mind doing written assignments.	1	2	3	4
24. It is easy for me to tell about the things I know.	1	2	3	4
25. If I understand a problem, I like to help someone else understand it, too.	1	2	3	4
26. I enjoy helping others learn while I learn.	1	2	3	4
27. I understand what I have learned better when I am involved in making something.	1	2	3	4
28. The things I write on paper sound better than when I say them.	1	2	3	4
29. I find it easier to remember what I have heard than what I have read.	1	2	3	4
30. It is fun to learn with classmates, but it is hard to study with them.	1	2	3	4

Appendix 6.1: *The Yes I Can! Model Learning Style Survey* (cont.)

Learning Style Survey Scoresheet

The numbers in the boxes below correspond to the numbers of the survey questions. Insert the number of your response (1, 2, 3, or 4) beside the question number in the boxes below. Then add up the response numbers to calculate the total for each learning style. The highest total indicates your major learning style, and the next highest indicates your minor learning style.

Visual	
Survey Q 4	
Survey Q 7	
Survey Q 13	
Survey Q 14	
Survey Q 20	
Total:	

Individual	
Survey Q 3	
Survey Q 9	
Survey Q 16	
Survey Q 19	
Survey Q 30	
Total:	

Auditory	
Survey Q 2	
Survey Q 8	
Survey Q 11	
Survey Q 15	
Survey Q 29	
Total:	

Group	
Survey Q 12	
Survey Q 17	
Survey Q 21	
Survey Q 25	
Survey Q 26	
Total:	

Kinesthetic (Hands-On)	
Survey Q 1	
Survey Q 10	
Survey Q 18	
Survey Q 22	
Survey Q 27	
Total:	

Expressive	
Survey Q 5	
Survey Q 6	
Survey Q 23	
Survey Q 24	
Survey Q 28	
Total:	

Highest total identifies your major learning style.	Second highest total indicates your minor learning style.
Major Learning Style:	**Minor Learning Style:**

Appendix 6.2

Sample Individual Learning Plan

Unit: _Cells_

Name: _Sophie_

Learning Style(s): _Visual and Group_

Standard: _Identify the function of the major plant and animal cellular organelles_

Baseline Activities for the Whole Class:

✓	Activity	Points earned	Points possible
	Cell notes *Microsoft Powerpoint®*		10
	Cell functions *Microsoft Powerpoint®*		10

Notes: _____

_____

Assessment:

✓	Activity	Points earned	Points possible
	Cell *Jeopardy!®*		10
	Cell Indicator Test		30

Baseline Activities: _____ / _____ pts. _____ %

Individual Activities: _____ / _____ pts. _____ %

Assessment: _____ / _____ pts. _____ %

Total: _____

Appendix 6.2: Sample Individual Learning Plan (cont.)

Individual Activity Options (by learning style)

Directions: Circle your choices for activities on. ___*cells*_____

Visual	Auditory	Group	Kinesthetic	Expressive	Individual
Study the online animal and plant cell comparison. Create a concept map detailing the main differences between plant and animal cells.	Use flashcards to conduct a question-and-answer session with a partner on cell structure and function. Using the Cell Structure and Function Flashcards, carry out Q-and-A with a partner and verify that each person is knowledgeable of cell organelles and functions.	Create cell models using the online cell gallery. Each group member chooses one cell example and constructs a model of the chosen cell type. Your group will share the model with the class and discuss key differences of the cell types.	Create a cell flip chart of cell organelles and functions. See *Cell Flip Chart* supplemental materials.	Writing and discussion topic—"How can we keep our cells healthy?" Lead a discussion or write a journal entry that includes at least five methods of keeping cells healthy. Include information on at least three different types of cells.	Complete the textbook review questions.
10 points	10 points	20 points	20 points	10 points	20 points
Cell explorer Complete an interactive lesson describing cell organelles and their functions. Create your own visual aid of the organelles discussed in the activity.	View the following video: *Biology: The Science of Life: The Living Cell.* Work with a partner to summarize your findings from the video.	Visit the "Human Cheek Cell Lab." Use the "Human Cheek Cell Lab" supplemental materials and discuss your findings with your group.	Create a cell mobile. Research a website that provides instructions on constructing a cell mobile.	Cell organelle poetry. Create a poem describing cell organelles and their functions.	Cells interactive test practice. Complete the interactive quiz online. Show teacher quiz results.
10 points	15 points	25 points	25 points	20 points	20 points
Virtual cell webpage tour. Use the link below for information to complete an online worksheet.	Watch *Cells: The Basic Units of Life* and complete the interactive video quiz.			Cell rap or jingle. Write and perform a rap or jingle about different types of cells and their functions. Include *bone, muscle, epithelial, nerve,* and *liver* cells.	Complete the cell organelles worksheet. Use available resources to complete the worksheet. See cell organelle worksheet supplemental materials.
24 points	20 points			20 points	20 points

Appendix 6.2: Sample Individual Learning Plan *(cont.)*

Unit: *Classroom environment*

Name: *Jackson*

Learning Style(s): *Visual and Group*

Standard: *Enhance teaching skills to increase effectiveness in the classroom; discuss and devise plans for improving the classroom environment*

Baseline Activities for the Whole Class:

✓	Activity	Points earned	Points possible
	Classroom environment discussion		10

Notes: _____

_____

Assessment:

✓	Activity	Points earned	Points possible
	Presentation of classroom environment strategies		10

Baseline Activities: _____ / _____ pts. _____ %

Individual Activities: _____ / _____ pts. _____ %

Assessment: _____ / _____ pts. _____ %

Total: _____

Appendix 6.2: Sample Individual Learning Plan (cont.)

Individual Activity Options (by learning style)

Directions: Circle your choices for activities on *creating a positive classroom environment*

Visual	Auditory	Group	Kinesthetic	Expressive	Individual
Read "How to Find Ways to Organize a Classroom Environment." Jot down a few notes to share with group.	Show *Classroom Environment* video clip. Share a few tips with the group.	Group discussion on topic: "Rewards that work." Create a list of applicable rewards.	Make a sticker chart. Make a sticker chart to monitor assignment progress.	Write a letter to parents. Create a letter to send home to parents informing them of your role this semester as their child's teacher.	Read *Top 10 Teaching Strategies* book. Create a summary of classroom environment tips.
10 points	10 points	10 points	15 points	10 points	10 points
Read "Are Your Students High-Maintenance?" from *Teacher Magazine*. Read article and develop your own plan of reducing repeated questions and requests.	Show *Survivor: The Middle School Classroom—Part II.* Watch video clip and share tips with others.	Group discussion on topic: "Time Management Strategies." Discuss good time management strategies to use in your classrooms and to share with the entire group.	Make note cards or craft sticks. Create note cards or craft sticks with each student's name for random questioning, group making, etc.	Make a creative display of rules, policies, and procedures.	Write on the topic of "Classroom Environment" in a portfolio or journal entry.
15 points	10 points	10 points	10 points	15 points	10 points
Read classroom environment web links and concept map. Choose an article of interest and create a concept map detailing your findings.		Group discussion on topic: "Rules—Short, Sweet, and Effective." Discuss your classroom rules. Talk about how you have stated them positively and briefly and how you are consistent in using them.	Make a creative display of rules, policies, and procedures.		Write a classroom management book. Research classroom environment tips.
15 points		10 points	15 points		10 points

Appendix 6.3

Individual Learning Plan Template

Unit: _____

Name: _____

Learning Style(s): _____

Standard: _____

Baseline Activities for the Whole Class:

✓	Activity	Points earned	Points possible

Notes: _____

_____

Assessment:

✓	Activity	Points earned	Points possible

Baseline Activities: _____ / _____ pts. _____ %

Individual Activities: _____ / _____ pts. _____ %

Assessment: _____ / _____ pts. _____ %

Total: _____

Appendix 6.3: Individual Learning Plan Template (cont.)

Individual Activity Options (by learning style)

Directions: Circle your choices for activities on _____

Visual	Auditory	Group	Kinesthetic	Expressive	Individual

Appendix 6.4

Individual Standard Log Templates

Standard or indicator:	Assessment used	Date offered	Date mastered
	Pre-test		X
	Verbal quiz		
	Clicker review		
	Post-test		
	Unit exam		

Standard or indicator:	Assessment used	Date offered	Date mastered
	Pre-test		X
	Verbal quiz		
	Clicker review		
	Post-test		
	Unit exam		

Standard or indicator:	Assessment used	Date offered	Date mastered
	Pre-test		X
	Verbal quiz		
	Clicker review		
	Post-test		
	Unit exam		

The Yes I Can! Model Student Feedback Survey

These are the results from a survey gathered in Spring 2008. Some students (depending on their age) had been involved with The Yes I Can! Model since 2004. This survey was created using SurveyMonkey (http://www.surveymonkey.com).

Question	Student answer
1. Are you male or female?	Male – 45%, Female – 54.9%
2. What is your grade level?	9th – 0% 11th – 40.8% 10th – 26.8% 12th – 32.4%
3. Activities in class were appropriate for my learning styles.	Yes – 95.8% No – 4.2%
4. Individual work activities deepened my understanding of the topics being learned.	Yes - 87.7% No – 12.3%
5. Using learning styles to customize my education was beneficial for me.	Yes – 82.4% No – 17.6%
6. Knowing how I learned material best helped me in other classes.	Yes – 63.0% No – 37.0%
7. I prefer having choices in how I learn the topic presented versus conventional learning methods (notes, lectures, tests, etc.)	Yes – 93.1% No – 6.9%
8. Using learning styles to customize my learning helped me to better prepare for the science assessment, to be more motivated, and to approach the assessment with a more positive attitude.	Yes – 69.0% No – 31.0%
9. If I could change one thing about the learning plans, it would be:	*"I want to use this information in my other classes."* *"We have a lot of options for individual work, but I want even more!"* *"I learned more in this class because of the way the lesson plans were set up. I would hope that more teachers would adjust their teaching to each student's specific needs."*
10. My favorite individual learning activities were:	*"I did very well learning with groups and seeing what other people thought. I liked doing certain activities of my choice that interested me instead of doing something boring."* *"Discussions, because the teacher always welcomed us and asked for our input and opinions...it was refreshing to be respected."* *"I am not the type of person that can learn with notes and lectures. I only learn by interacting. This class was great for that!"*

References Cited

Allen, K. and J. Scheve. 2008 *The Yes I Can! Training Manual.* Garnett, KS: Dawg Prints.

Angelo, T. A. A teacher's dozen: Fourteen general, research-based principles for improving higher learning in our classrooms. *AAHE Bulletin*, 45(8), April 1993.

Armour-Thomas, E., C. Clay, R. Domanico, K. Bruno, and B. Allen. 1989. *An outlier study of elementary and middle schools in New York City: Final report.* NY: New York City Board of Education.

ASCD. 2006 Annual Conference Blog. http://ascd.typepad.com/annualconference/.

Bornstein, M. H. Frames of Mind: The theory of multiple intelligences by Howard Gardner. *Journal of Aesthetic Education*, University of Illinois Press. 20, 2. Summer 1986:120–122. http://www.jstor.org/stable/3332707

Brown, M. W. and C. Hurd. 1942. *The Runaway Bunny.* NY: HarperCollins, (2005.)

Brualdi, A. C. 1996. Multiple intelligences: Gardner's theory. *Eric Digest*. Washington, D.C.: ERIC Clearinghouse on Assessment and Evaluation

Burke, K., F. Guastello, R. Dunn, S. A. Griggs, T. M. Beasley, J. Gemake, R. Sinatra, and B. Lewthwaite. 1998. Relationship(s) between global-format and analytic-format learning-style assessments based on the Dunn and Dunn model. *National Forum of Applied Educational Research Journal*, 13(1), 76-96.

Carbo, M. 1988. Reading style inventory. NY: Learning Research.

Carbo, M., R. Dunn, and K. Dunn. 1986. *Teaching students to read through their individual learning styles.* NJ: Prentice-Hall.

Checkley, K. 1997. The first seven…and the eighth: A conversation with Howard Gardner. ASCD. FirstSevenAndEighth-1.pdf.

Combat Poverty Agency. 1998. Position paper for the National Forum on Early Childhood Education. Available at: 1998_Paper_NationalForumEarlyChildhoodEducation.pdf.

Dryden, G. and J. Vohs. 1999. The learning revolution. http://www.thelearningweb.net/personalthink.html, retrieved January 5, 2009.

Dunn, R. 2007. Interview at Ball State University. Reviewed in the *Institute for Learning Styles Journal* Vol. 1, Fall 2007.

Dunn, R., K. Burke, and S. Rundle. 2007. Elementary Learning Style Assessment (ELSA). Pittsford, NY: Learning Concepts, Inc.

Dunn, R. and T. DeBello. 1999. Improved test scores, attitudes, and behaviors in America's schools: Supervisor's success stories. Westport, CT: Praeger.

Dunn, R. and K. Dunn. 1978. Learning style questionnaire. NY: St. John's University, Center for the Study of Learning and Teaching Styles.

————. 1992. *Teaching elementary students through their individual learning styles*. Boston, MA: Allyn & Bacon.

————. 1993. *Teaching secondary students through their individual learning styles: Practical approaches for grades 7–12*. Boston, MA: Allyn & Bacon.

Dunn, R., K. Dunn, and J. Perrin. 1994. *Teaching young children through their individual learning styles: Practical approaches for grades K–2*. Boston, MA: Allyn & Bacon.

Dunn, R., K. Dunn, and G. E. Price. 1975–1996. Learning Style Inventory, Lawrence, Kansas: Price Systems, Inc.; referenced in Ball, A.L. The secrets of learning styles—your child's and your own. *Redbook*. (1982, Nov.). 160, 1, 73–76.

————. 1979, 1980, 1982, 1990, 1996. Productivity Environmental Preference Survey (PEPS).

Dunn, R. and S. A. Griggs. 1988. Learning styles: A quiet revolution in American secondary schools. Reston, VA.: National Association of Secondary School Principals.

————. 2003. Synthesis of the Dunn and Dunn learning-style model research: Who, what, when, where, and so what? Jamaica, NY: St. John's University, Center for the Study of Learning and Teaching Styles.

Dunn, R., A. Theis, and A. Honigsfeld. 2001. Synthesis of the Dunn and Dunn learning-style model research: Analysis from a neuropsychological perspective. NY: St. John's University, Center for the Study and Learning and Teaching Styles.

Fathers, Founding. 2007. The United States Constitution. Standard Publications, Incorporated, September.

Ferguson, R. 1991. Paying for public education: New evidence on how and why money matters. *Harvard Journal of Education*, 28, 25–38.

Fleming, N. D. 1993. From teaching to learning. The Centre for Teaching and Learning presents Neil D. Fleming (Lincoln University, New Zealand). http://web4.uwindsor.ca/units/ctl/main.nsf/main/A38CDB85B51 D673B852574010062FBA4?OpenDocument

Fleming, N. D. 2001. *Teaching and learning styles: VARK strategies*. Privately printed.

Fleming, N. D. and C. Mills. 1992. Not another inventory, rather a catalyst for reflection, to improve the academy, Vol. 11, 1992, 137.

Gardner, H. 1987. Beyond IQ: Education and human development. *Harvard Educational Review* 57, 2. 187–193.

————. 1983. *Frames of mind: The theory of multiple intelligences*. NY: Basic Books.

———. 2006. Howard Gardner: Hobbs professor of cognition and education. Harvard Graduate School of Education. http://www.howardgardner.com.

———. 1993. *Multiple intelligences: The theory in practice*. NY: Basic Books.

———. 1991. *The unschooled mind, how children think and how schools should teach*. NY: Basic Books, Inc.

Gregorc, A. 1999–present. F. Gregorc Associates, Inc. http://gregorc.com/, retrieved January 5, 2009.

Gregorc, A. 1986. *An adult's guide to style*. Maynard, MA: Gabriel Systems.

———. 1982. *Gregorc style delineator: Development, technical and administrative manual*. Maynard, MA: Gabriel Systems, Inc.

———. 1979. Learning/teaching styles: Potent forces behind them. *Educational Leadership*, 234–236.

Guastello, E. F. and R. Dunn. 1998. *Our wonderful learning style*. NY: St. John's University, Center for the Study of Learning and Teaching Styles.

Kettelkamp, T. 1999. Theory of multiple intelligence, Gardner 1983. New York State Recreation and Parks State Conference. March 9.

Kugel, P. 1993. How professors develop as teachers. Studies in higher education, 18:3.

Levine, M. 2006. Helping a mind become defined. Chautauqua Lecture series (WQLN); Sept. 21

Looney Tunes. 1948. Warner Bros. Pictures.

Mawhinney, T. S. 2002. The effects of teaching prescriptions on the self-assessed teaching styles and beliefs of secondary school teachers. (Doctoral dissertations, St. John's University, 2002).

Missere, N. and R. Dunn. 2007. Learning in Vogue, Elements of Style! (LIVES!) Pittsford, NY: Learning Concepts, Inc. Available at: http://lives.learningstyles.net/test/index.php?lang=1

Morgan, J. 2008. Vark Learning Styles. http://www.getallinformation.com/academics-learning/article5136.htm, retrieved Feb. 2, 2009.

Nieter, V. and R. Dunn. 2008. Observational Preschool/Primary Assessment of Learning Styles (OPALS). Pittsford, NY: Learning Concepts, Inc.

Ortman, C. L. Learning styles of the academically talented. (Honors thesis, Ball State University, 1987). O78_1987OrtmanConnieL.pdf.

Pallotta, J. 1999. *The Hershey's® milk chocolate bar fractions book*. New York, NY: Scholastic Cartwheel Books.

Perrin, J. 1981. *Learning style inventory*. Privately printed.

Press, Associated, L. D. Boccardi. 2000. *The Associated Press stylebook and briefing on media law*. Revised. Basic Books, January 15.

Rundle, S. and R. Dunn. 1996–2000. Building Excellence (BE). Pittsford, NY: Performance Concepts, Inc.

Sanders, W. and S. Horn. 1998. Research findings from the Tennessee Value-Added Assessment System (TVAAS) database: Implications for educational evaluation and research. *Journal of Personnel Evaluation in Education*, 12(3), 247-256.

Scherer, M. 2006. Celebrate strengths, nurture affinities: A conversation with Mel Levine. *Educational Leadership*, 64, 1. 8–15.

Sesame Street. http://www.sesamestreet.org/home.

Seuss, Dr. 1938. *The 500 hats of Bartholomew Cubbins*. Vanguard Press.

Shearer, B. 1987. MIDAS™ test. M.I. Research and Consulting.

Stevens, J. 1995. *Tops and bottoms*. Orlando, FL: Harcourt Brace & Co.

Sullivan, M. 1996–97. A meta-analysis of experimental research studies based on the Dunn and Dunn learning styles model and its relationship to academic achievement and performance. *National Forum of Applied Educational Research Journal*, 10(1), 3-10.

Taylor, R. T. 2002. Multiple intelligences product grid. Curriculum Design Online. http://www.rogertaylor.com

The National Teaching and Learning Forum. http://www.ntlf.com/, May 1998 Vol. 7, No. 4; retrieved Jan. 16, 2009.

The Physics Classroom. http://www.physicsclassroom.com/.

Thies, A. 1979. A brain-behavior analysis of learning styles. In *Student learning styles: Diagnosing and prescribing programs*. Reston, VA: National Association of Secondary School Principals, 55–61.

———. 2003. Implication of neuroscience and neuropsychology for the Dunn and Dunn Learning-Style Theory. In *Synthesis of the Dunn and Dunn Learning-Style Model research: Who, what, when, where, and so what?* Dunn, R. S., and Griggs, S. A., eds. 2003. 49–54. New York: St. John's University.

———. 2000. The neuropsychology of learning styles. *National Forum of Applied Educational Research Journal*, 13(1). 50–62.

Topping, K. J. 2001. *Peer assisted learning: A practical guide for teachers*. Cambridge MA: Brookline Books.

Twain, M. 1885. *The adventures of Huckleberry Finn (Tom Sawyer's comrade)*. Harper & Brothers. (2004.)

Additional Resources

Websites:

Curriculum Design for Excellence, Inc./Dr. Roger Taylor
Dr. Taylor has several webinars posted on this website, which is a professional development resource. Available at: **http://www.rogertaylor. com/**

Discovery Education
This subscription website offers numerous resources, video clips, lesson plans, and online tools across content areas. Available at:
http://www.discoveryeducation.com/index.cfm?bluSearchluit=true

Institute for Learning Styles Research
This website is devoted to providing training and community resources for evaluating Learning Styles. Available at: **http://learningstyles.net**

JeopardyLabs
This website allows you to create a customized *Jeopardy*® template. The games you make can be played online. Available at:
http://www.jeopardylabs.com

The Learning Web
This is an online edition of *The new learning revolution and the seven keys to unlock it* by Gordon Dryden and Jeannette Vos. Available at:
http://www.thelearningweb.net

Multiple Intelligences Inventory
A part of the Learning Disabilities Resource Community, this website offers an online inventory survey to determine multiple intelligences. Available at:
http://www.ldrc.ca/projects/miinventory/miinventory.php

Project Zero
Howard Gardner's official website is located at this Harvard Graduate School of Education research project page. Available at: **http://pzweb.harvard. edu/index.cfm;** also, **http://www.howardgardner.com**

SurveyMonkey
This is a web-based survey tool that allows you to design, administer, and tabulate your own customized survey. Available at:
http://www.surveymonkey.com

VARK: A guide to learning styles
This site offers the VARK questionnaire and offers suggestions for useful materials. Available at: **http://www.vark-learn.com/english/page. asp?p=questionnaire**